Catch Me a Colobus

Gerald Durrell was born in Jamshedpur, India, in 1925. In 1928 his family returned to England and in 1933 they went to live on the Continent. Eventually they settled on the island of Corfu, where they lived until 1939. During this time he made a special study of zoology, and kept a large number of the local wild animals as pets.

In 1945 he joined the staff of Whipsnade Zoo as a student keeper, and in 1947 financed, organized and led an animal-collecting expedition to the Cameroons. This gave rise to the first of his immensely popular books, *The Overloaded Ark*. Since then he has been on other expeditions to the Cameroons, British Guiana, Paraguay and Argentina.

In 1958 he founded the Jersey Wildlife Preservation Trust, and in 1961 went to New Zealand, Australia and Malaya – the expedition which formed the basis of *Two in the Bush*. In 1965 he went to Sierra Leone with a BBC film unit to film *Catch Me a Colobus*, an episode which figures largely in the present book. His first novel, *Rosy is My Relative*, was published in 1968.

D0310051

Catch Me a Colobus

Gerald Durrell

Drawings by Edward Mortelmans

Fontana/Collins

First published in 1972 by William Collins Sons & Co Ltd
First issued in Fontana Books 1975
Eighth impression June 1983

Made and printed in Great Britain by
William Collins Sons & Co Ltd, Glasgow

This book is for five stalwart members of my staff whose hard work, dedication and cheerfulness (even in moments of gloom and despondency) have helped me so much. Without their staunch backing I could have achieved little or nothing. They are Catha Weller, Betty Boizard, Jeremy Mallinson, John (Shep) Mallet, and John (Long John) Hartley.

Author's Note

As the incidents in this book cover a period of about seven years and I have had to do a lot of pruning and grafting, some of them do not appear in the exact order in which they happened. This has been done purely to make the book run more smoothly, so if any of my readers notice that certain things are not necessarily in sequence they will understand why.

My thanks are due to Messrs. Rupert Hart-Davis for permission to use the extract from *Menagerie Manor* on page 12.

I Wash and Brush Up

Dear Mr Durrell,
I have frequently wondered about kangaroo pouches . . .

When I come back from an expedition abroad I always have a sense of great excitement at seeing the zoo again: the new cages that have been constructed in my absence from what had been mere drawings, the new animals that have arrived, the animals which have given birth; to be greeted by the discordant cries of joy from the various animals that recognize you and are pleased to see you back. Generally, it's a very pleasant and exciting homecoming.

But on this occasion I had been on a fairly prolonged trip to Australia, New Zealand and Malaya, and on my return I found, to my consternation, that my precious zoo was looking shabby and unkempt. Not only that, but I soon discovered that it was almost bankrupt. After all the hard work and money that I had put into it, it was rather like being kicked in the solar plexus. Far from being able to relax after what had been a fairly hectic trip, I had to set to with the utmost rapidity to see what I could do to save the zoo.

The first thing I did, of course, was take over the management of the place myself, and then offer the job of Deputy Director to Jeremy Mallinson, who had been with the zoo since its inception. I knew of his immense integrity and of his deep love for the animals in his care. Moreover, he had worked in every section of the zoo and therefore knew most of the problems involved. To my infinite relief he accepted the job. Then I had a meeting with the heads of all the other sections and explained the situation to them. I said that it was more than likely that the zoo might have to close down, but, that if they were prepared to stay with me and work as hard as they could for a pittance, there was a good possibility that we might be able to pull it out of the mire. To their everlasting credit they all agreed to do this. So at least I knew that the animals would not suffer and would be well looked after.

My next job was to try and find a good administrative secretary. This was not as easy as it sounds. I advertised, and specified in the advertisement that a knowledge of shorthand, typing, and, most important of all, book-keeping, were essential. Somewhat to my surprise I got a flood of applicants. On interviewing them, I found that half of them couldn't add two and two and make four, and very few of them knew what a typewriter even looked like. One young man even went so far as to say that he had applied for the job because he thought he could pick it up as he went along. After interviewing about twenty of these morons I was beginning to lose hope. Then we came to one Catha Weller. She waltzed into my office for her interview, diminutive, rotund, with sparkling green eyes and a comforting smile. She explained that her husband had just been transferred to Jersey and that she had had to give up her job in London, which she had had for the last seventeen years. Yes, she knew how to do book-keeping, shorthand and typing — the lot. I looked at Jacquie and Jacquie looked at me. We both knew instinctively that a miracle had happened; we had found exactly what we wanted. So, within a few days, Catha Weller was installed, trying to make some sort of order out of the chaos of book-keeping that had accumulated during my absence abroad.

The zoo, at that time, had two debts: one of twenty thousand pounds, which was the money that I had borrowed and which had been used for the original construction work, and a local overdraft and creditors amounting to another fourteen thousand pounds. My next problem, of course, was the difficult one of how to get sufficient finance to keep the zoo on an even keel in order that it should survive. This occupied me for some considerable time. During all this time Jeremy, being new to his job, had to keep coming to consult me about various animal problems, and Catha about various financial matters, all of which were new to her, and this, combined with the worry of trying to think of a way of saving the zoo, drove me into the very depths of depression. So, in spite of my protests, Jacquie called in our doctor.

'I'm not ill,' I protested. 'It's just worry. Can't you give me a jab of something to keep me going?'

'I'll do better than that,' said Mike. 'I'll give you some tablets to take.'

So he prescribed a bottle of rather lurid looking little capsules, of which I was supposed to take one a day. Little did he or I know that by doing this he was making the most important gesture towards saving the zoo.

Now two of our dearest and oldest friends on the island are Hope and Jimmy Platt. Jimmy spent most of his time in London, but Hope was a constant visitor to the zoo and would frequently pop up for a drink. She happened to come up one evening when I had, quite by mistake, taken two of my tranquillizers instead of one. The result was that I looked and sounded as though I was in the last stages of inebriation. Hope is a large and formidable woman, and she frowned at me as I staggered across the room to greet her.

'What's the matter with you?' she inquired, with all the authority of fourteen stone. 'Have you been hitting the bottle?'

'No,' I replied, 'I wish I had. It's these damned tranquillizers. I took two instead of one.'

'Tranquillizers?' said Hope, incredulously. 'What on earth are you taking tranquillizers for?'

'Sit down and let me get you a drink, and I'll tell you all about it,' I said.

So for the next hour I poured out my tale of woe to Hope. At the end of it she heaved herself massively out of the chair and stood up to go.

'We'll soon put a stop to this,' she said firmly. 'I'm not having you taking tranquillizers at your age. I'm going to see Jimmy about it.'

'But, I don't see why Jimmy should be worried . . .' I began.

'You listen to Mama,' said Hope. 'I'll speak to Jimmy.'

And so she did. The next thing was a phone call from Jimmy. Would I please go round and see him and explain the matter. So I went round and told him how I had planned, originally, that once the zoo was self-supporting I was going to turn it into a Trust, but that it would be impossible to start a Trust carrying such an enormous debt. Jimmy agreed entirely, and sat brooding for a while.

'Well there's only one thing to be done,' he said at last, 'and that's to launch a public appeal. First of all, I'll give you two thousand pounds in order to tide you over your present difficulties, and I shall also contribute two thousand pounds to the appeal to encourage other people. If the appeal is a success, we can think again.'

To say that I was overwhelmed would be putting it mildly, and I went back to the zoo in a sort of daze. It really seemed as though there might be a chance of saving the place after all.

Launching an appeal is not quite as easy as it sounds. Neither is every appeal necessarily successful. But here our local paper, the *Evening Post,* which had always been our ally, gave us a most wonderful write-up about what we had done in the past, and explained our aims for the future. The appeal was launched and, in what seemed like a miraculously short space of time, we had raised twelve thousand pounds. I think the two donations that touched me most were the one from a small boy, of five shillings, which must have been his week's pocket money, and another contribution of five pounds from the staff of the Jersey Zoo. This money was going to be the working capital of the Trust and therefore it could not be used for all the vital jobs that needed to be done in the zoo itself.

We now came to the second part of Jimmy's stratagem. Both he and I agreed that the Trust could not be formed unless the matter of the original loan were cleared up. The Trust could then be launched with the twelve thousand pounds in hand, which would give it a good start, though still not good enough to allow for any large-scale rebuilding or development. So I, personally, agreed to pay back the twenty thousand pounds owing to an increasingly restive bank out of my book royalties, and hand over the zoo and its contents to the Trust. This was done, and the Jersey Wildlife Preservation Trust came into being and officially took over the zoo, with myself acting as Honorary Director of both the Trust and the zoo. We chose a group of active people who were sympathetic towards our aims to act as our Council, and were delighted when Lord Jersey agreed to become our President. We chose, as our emblem, the Dodo, that large waddling pigeon-like bird that had once inhabited the island of Mauritius, and which was exterminated with great rapidity as soon as the island had been discovered. We felt that it symbolized the way in which a species can be wiped off the face of the earth in a remarkably short space of time by the thoughtlessness and greed of man.

But we were not out of the woods yet. It was still a very trying time, and I was still living on tranquillizers, unbeknownst to Hope Platt. For, at the same time as all this was going on, I was trying to write a book. This is a task that I view with abhorrence at the best of times, but now it was imperative, for I had twenty thousand pounds to pay back to the bank and the only way I could earn the money was by writing.

The book was called *Menagerie Manor,* and in it I explained why I wanted a zoo in the first place, and why I wanted the zoo eventually to become a Trust. I can do no better, I think, to explain it now than to quote what I wrote then:

'I did not want a simple, straightforward zoo, with the ordinary run of animals: the idea behind my zoo was to aid in the preservation of animal life. All over the world various species are being exterminated or cut down to remnants of their former numbers by the spread of civilization. Many of the larger species are of commercial or tourist value, and, as such, are receiving the most attention. Yet, scattered about all over the world, are a host of fascinating small mammals, birds and reptiles, and scant attention is being paid to their preservation, as they are neither edible nor wearable, and of little interest to the tourist who demands lions and rhinos. A great number of these are island fauna, and as such their habitat is small. The slightest interference with this, and they will vanish forever: the casual introduction of rats, say, or pigs could destroy one of these island species within a year. The obvious answer to this whole problem is to see that the creature is adequately protected in the wild state so that it does not become extinct, but this is often easier said than done. However, while pressing for this protection, there is another precaution that can be taken, and that is to build up under controlled conditions breeding stocks of these creatures in parks or zoos, so that, should the worst happen and the species become extinct in the wild state, you have, at least, not lost it forever. Moreover, you have a breeding stock from which you can glean the surplus animals and reintroduce them into their original homes at some future date. This, it has always seemed to me, should be the main function of any zoo, but it is only recently that the majority of zoos have woken up to this fact and tried to do anything about it. I wanted this to be the main function of my zoo.'

The problems of forming the Trust were greater and more complex than I had anticipated. They ranged from what subscription we should charge to members not so large that people could not afford to *become* members, yet not so small that it would be of little benefit to us down to details like what pamphlets we were going to publish to explain our aims and objects, and how these pamphlets were to be distributed. Over the years I have received a great number of letters about my books, and all of these had been answered and copies had been kept. So now all these people were circularized with a pamphlet and an enrolment form and, to my great delight, the vast majority of them joined the Trust immediately. When the new book, *Menagerie Manor*, was published it proved very popular (fortunately for me), and in it I asked any readers to join the Trust. So we got a fresh batch of members. By now we had some seven hundred and fifty Trust members dotted about in all parts of the world. It was particularly encouraging to think that people in countries as far away as Australia, South Africa and the United States were supporting a project which they might never even see.

At that time we were all working flat out for, although things were still fairly dicey, we could at least see, distantly on the horizon, some sign of success. To say that we were exhausted at the end of each day was an understatement.

At that time I started receiving a spate of telephone calls, and these generally happened at the most irritating times. In the middle of lunch, for instance, I was called to the telephone – a long distance call from a woman in Torquay whose tortoise had just given birth to eggs. She wanted to know what to do with them. On another occasion, a woman wanted to know how to clip her budgerigar's toenails. But the telephone call that really put the lid on it came at eleven o'clock one night when I was drowsing in front of the fire. It was a long distance call from up north: a Lord McDougall wanted to speak to me. Thinking, in my innocence, that perhaps he wanted to give a large sum of money for the Trust, I asked the operator to put him through. When he came on the line it became immediately obvious that his lordship had imbibed wisely but in too great a quantity.

'Ish that Durrell?' he wanted to know.

'Yes,' I said.

'Ah,' he said. 'Now, you are the one man in England who can help me. I have a bird.'

I groaned inwardly. It was sure to be another budgerigar, I thought.

'I own . . . a fleet of ships,' he said, enunciating with great difficulty, 'and one of my captains had thish . . . bird fly on board and he has jus' brought it to me. Now . . . I want to know if you can help it?'

'Well, what sort of bird is it?' I inquired.

'It's a shweet little thing,' he said.

As a zoological description this left much to be desired.

'I mean, what sort of size or shape is it?'

'Well . . . it's a very shmall greyish-brown bird, with a whitish breast,' he said. 'Very tiny feet . . . *very* tiny feet. . . . *Remarkably* tiny feet, in fact. . . .'

'I think it must be a Stormy Petrel,' I said. 'They do, quite frequently, fly on board ships.'

'I will immediately charter a train and shend it to you if you can shave it,' said his lordship lavishly.

I explained, at great length, that this would be quite useless. These tiny birds spend most of their lives at sea, feeding on minute forms of animal life, and are almost impossible to keep in captivity. In any case, even if he did send the bird to me, by the time it arrived it would most assuredly be dead.

'I will shpare no expenshe whatshoever,' said his lordship.

At that moment the telephone was torn from his grasp and a girl with a very county voice said, 'Mr Durrell?'

'Yes,' I said.

'I do apologize for Daddy,' she said, 'but I'm afraid he's not quite himself. Please don't take any notice.'

The telephone was wrenched from her, and his lordship came on again.

'I will do anything,' he said. 'Fasht cars, planes, anything you like to get the bird to you.'

'I'm afraid even if you got it to me, I could do nothing for it,' I said.

'Here I'll put you on to my captain; he knows all about it,' said his lordship.

A dour Scottish voice came on the phone.

'Good evening, sir.'

'Good evening,' I said.

'You say you think the bird's a Stormy Petrel?' asked the captain.

'Yes,' I said, 'I'm almost certain. But in any case, the only thing to do is to keep it warm and in a dark place, send it out on one of your ships tomorrow. As soon as they are as far out to sea as they think necessary – two or three miles, perhaps – they can then let it go.'

'I see,' he said. 'I must apologize for worrying you at this hour of night, but his lordship insisted.'

'Yes,' I said. 'I . . . er . . . I understand the circumstances perfectly.'

'His lordship, you understand,' went on the Scots voice, 'is a very kind man, and very, very keen on birds, but he's not quite himself tonight.'

'So I gather,' I said. 'I wish I was in the same state.'

'Er . . . yessir,' said the captain. 'Well, er, I'll be saying goodnight, then, sir.'

'Goodnight,' I said, and put the phone back.

'What on earth was all that about?' said Jacquie.

'A drunken lord, trying to send me a Stormy Petrel,' I said, sinking into my chair.

'Really!' she said, angrily, 'this has got to stop. We must get an ex-directory number.'

And so we did, and since then this spate of extraordinary telephone calls has mercifully ceased.

The following morning I related this incident to Catha, and she was amused though sympathetic.

'Have you heard the story about Jeremy and the mole?' she inquired.

'No,' I said, 'I haven't. What is it?'

Apparently, Jeremy had been driving the zoo lorry from the mammal house through the two great arches that guard the courtyard, carrying the debris of the day's cleaning out. When he reached the second arch he saw, crawling across the gravel, a mole. He immediately clamped on his brakes, stepped out of the lorry, and approached the mole with the idea that he would carry it to an adjoining field where it would be safe. When he got closer he discovered that the mole was not only very dead, but attached to a length of twine, and it was being slowly pulled across the gravel. Following the twine to clear up this mystery, he found the entire bird staff at the end of it, pulling gently. The practical joker was Shep Mallet (known as Shep since, when he had first arrived, he had been nicknamed Shepton Mallet). He had not, for some time, played any practical jokes on people and I greeted this as a very good sign. It meant that the air of gloom and despondency, which I had found so prevalent on my return, had disappeared and was being replaced with hope and enthusiasm.

However, at this point, although hope and enthusiasm were things that were vitally needed, they had to be backed up with sufficient money. It was hard cash that we needed to rebuild cages that were by then five years old, and rebuild, moreover, not in a haphazard way but with some over-all plan in mind. Every day it seemed that cages had to be shored up when really they should have been pulled down and rebuilt. Among the smaller animals and birds this did not matter so much, but when it came to the larger and more dangerous creatures, the problem became acute. In spite of the help that I had had from Hope and Jimmy in setting up the Trust, we were still desperately short of money and, in particular, money to create satisfactory caging for those animals that could be potentially lethal if they escaped. This was brought home to me forcibly by certain events that followed each other in alarmingly quick succession.

At the far end of the mammal house, where the gorillas had their quarters, we had had a small collection box constructed, and above it a notice telling of the aims and objects of the Trust, in the hope that kindly members of the public would put donations in it. In due course they did. One lunchtime, when there happened to be nobody about, I went into the mammal house to have a look at a marmoset that was supposed to be pregnant. I saw to my alarm that the door on the orang-utan cage was open and hanging crookedly on its hinges. I hurried down there and, to my relief, found both the orang-utans still sitting in the cage, but Oscar, the elder orang-utan, must have found some sort of a tool in order to have wrenched the door open. Having done that, he had then explored the mammal house. The only thing of interest which he had found that he could detach easily and take back with him as a souvenir was the Jersey Wildlife Preservation Trust collecting box. As soon as he discovered that this rattled, he rattled it vigorously. Finding that the coins wouldn't come out of the slot, he'd soon tracked down the door at the back and wrenched it open. When I arrived on the scene he was sitting in a pile of half-crowns, sixpences and pennies. He was most irritated with me when I went into the cage, seized the box and picked up the money. I wasn't sure how much money there had been in the first place, so it was a little difficult, but I felt sure there must be some more hidden around in the straw which I had missed. Then I looked at Oscar and I noticed that his face was swollen and looked more puffy than usual.

'Oscar,' I said sternly, 'you've got some in your mouth. Give it to me.'

I held out my hand and, with the greatest reluctance, he spat out five half-crowns and about four sixpences.

'Is that the lot?' I demanded.

He just sat and looked at me with his little almond-shaped eyes. I put the money back in the box, climbed out of the cage, and made a temporary repair to the door. Then, just as I was leaving to go and tell our maintenance man that the door needed fixing properly, Oscar spat a defiant penny at me.

But the incident that really made us realize the importance of getting new ape cages done as quickly as possible was when the chimps got out. It was a Christmas Day, and we had invited Catha and her husband, Sam, over to have Christmas dinner with us. Christmas Day is the only day that the zoo closes, and it was extremely fortunate for us that all the staff were still in the zoo and had not

dispersed to their various Christmas dinners. Our turkey was done to a turn, the chestnut stuffing smelt marvellous, and all the vegetables were ready at a quarter to one, when the door burst open and a member of the staff rushed in, shouting, 'Mr D., Mr D., the chimps are out!' I'd had Cholmondley (or Chumley, as he was more commonly spelt) since he was quite a tiny baby, but even in those days, when he'd gone to do something disobedient and my mother had tried to stop him, he'd bitten her in the arm, which had necessitated seventeen stitches. Now he was almost as big and heavy as I was, so I had no wish to tangle with him or with Sheena, his wife, who was about the same size.

'Where are they?' I asked.

'They're just going into the courtyard.'

I rushed to the drawing-room window and looked out. There was Chumley walking along with Sheena, her arm draped affectionately over his shoulder, looking for all the world like an elderly couple enjoying a walk along the Bournemouth sea-front. Just at that moment Catha and Sam's car swept into the courtyard and came to a halt at the front door. Sheena was inclined to be a little nervous of this new apparition, but Chumley greeted it with hoots of delight. He knew all about cars as he had driven in them with me a number of times when he was a baby, and had thoroughly enjoyed watching the scenery and the passing traffic. He went up to the car, where Catha and Sam had wisely rolled up their windows, and banged on the glass in the hope that Catha would open up and give him a lift. However, she did no such thing.

I rushed downstairs, telling Jacquie to lock the flat door behind me, shut my office door, opened the door leading into the big main offices, and then flung open the front door. Chumley, on seeing me, gave several hoots of greeting and started ambling towards the houses. I scooted out through the office, opening the door that led into a passageway which, in turn, led to the stairs up to the staff quarters and to the big kitchen which served the café. I felt that if we could get the chimps in there we could trap them one way or another. I then went outside the house, round the back, in through the back door, and took up my stand peering through the crack of the door leading to the offices.

Chumley had decided he might as well pass the time of day with me and wish me a merry Christmas, so he was just walking in through the front door, followed by Sheena. They couldn't go anywhere but into the main office and this they did. It was the work of a moment to close the sliding doors on them; but I hoped that they would get into the back passageway as quickly as possible, as in the office were all the files and they could do a considerable amount of damage in a very short time. To my relief Chumley, finding that there was nobody in the office, did precisely that. But when he got into the back passage there was a choice between going along it and into the big kitchen, or upstairs to the staff living quarters. Chumley knew all about stairs, for when he was a baby our flat had been up several flights of them, and he thought that this flight might lead him to me. So up he went, followed by a somewhat dubious Sheena. Luckily, all the staff bedroom doors were shut, with the exception of one, and this was the one that the chimps naturally made for.

We followed at a respectful distance and, when they were safely inside, slammed the door on them and turned the key. Then we went outside, got ladders and climbed up to the windows of the room to see what they were doing. Chumley had discovered, with great satisfaction, that there was a basin and a cake of soap in the room. He had turned on both taps to the fullest extent and was busy washing his hands, a habit he had much enjoyed when young. Sheena, on the other hand, was bouncing up and down on the bed, clasping a pillow to her bosom. She then found out that, by digging her nails in and pulling hard, it was quite easy to burst a pillow with the most satisfactory result that clouds of feathers filled the air. So she burst both pillows and the room looked as though it was having a snowstorm. A large quantity of feathers drifted down and settled in the basin, thus effectively clogging it. The basin started to fill

and eventually overflowed, for Chumley by now had lost interest in it and he and Sheena were dismantling the bed with great thoroughness. When they came to the mattress they discovered that this, too, could be ripped open and the contents scattered about the room. Now the room was not only full of feathers but little bits of sorbo rubber, horse-hair, and so on. I had a hasty conference with Jeremy. We had one cage strong enough and big enough to put the two chimps in, but this was made of solid steel and required about six people to lift it, and I doubted whether, in fact, we could get it up the stairs to the staff quarters.

'The only thing to do is to try and get them down again,' said Jeremy. 'If we can get them to go along the corridor to the end there, where there are the two doors, we can trap them between the two doors and then manoeuvre the cage into place.'

We climbed up the ladders once again and peered in. Chumley had now found a coat-hanger and had managed to break a mirror with it. Sheena was still busily disembowelling the mattress with all the intentness of a world-famous surgeon doing a heart-transplant.

'If somebody were to open the door,' said Jeremy, 'he could nip across and lock himself in the bathroom. He'd be safe there. Then, perhaps, they'd go downstairs of their own accord.'

'Well, we can try it,' I said.

So a member of the staff went up, opened the door of the bedroom in which the chimps were disporting themselves, then whipped across the corridor and locked himself in the bathroom. The chimps, as I had suspected, were having far too good a time to wish to vacate their quarters. They merely glanced up when the door was opened and returned to their various activities. In Chumley's case he was collecting together as many feathers as he could and throwing them in the air, while Sheena was still busy on her operation and the mattress was looking as though it would not survive.

'I think there's only one thing to do,' said Jeremy. 'We'll have to hose them out.'

Now the curious thing was that, though both the chimps liked water to drink and to play with, they couldn't bear to get it on their bodies. On some nights, when they had refused to go into their bedroom, we had had to threaten them with the hosepipe, whereupon they went in like lambs. We though that this method might work equally well now.

The hosepipe was solemnly brought up and attached to the tap in the animal kitchen, and we broke a pane of glass in the window in order to stick the end through. Then the water was turned on full force and the jet directed into the room. The chimps looked up in astonishment at this dastardly attack and then, as the stream of water hit them, ran screaming out of the bedroom, down the stairs and into the passage. Here we had two other members of the staff waiting concealed. As soon as the chimps reached the right spot both doors in the passageway were slammed and they were neatly trapped in a small area where they could do no damage and from which they couldn't escape. I think we all felt relieved at this point, for chimps, being rather hysterical, extrovert creatures, quickly get over-excited and when over-excited could easily attack you. By this time both Sheena and Chumley were thoroughly over-excited, to say the least.

Our next job was to get the big iron cage and bring it down to one of the doors. This took a long time, for the cage had not been in use for ages and so was covered with stacks of timber and other materials which had accumulated in the workshop. Finally, however, we got it clear and six of us carried it and put it in position by the door. The sliding door of the cage was raised and then the door into the house carefully opened. The chimps were sitting there, dripping water from their fur, looking extremely belligerent. For an hour we tempted them with every delicacy we could think of to try to entice them into the cage, but nothing – not even out-of-season grapes – would make them enter it.

'What about a snake?' I said, for I knew that Chumley had a great fear of snakes.

'No, it won't work,' said Jeremy. 'At least, it will for Chumley, he'll go in for a snake. But Sheena won't; she's not a bit scared of them.'

'Well, it will have to be the hosepipe again,' I said gloomily. 'God knows what damage we've done already with water.'

So the hosepipe was carried round to the kitchen and attached to the tap. We then went to the other door, opened it, and directed a firm stream of water at the two chimps. They immediately rushed into the cage, the sliding iron door clanged shut, and they were safely prisoners once more. Together with Bert, our maintenance man, we went down to the chimps' cage to see exactly how they had managed to escape. They were kept behind thick interlink wire, which was strong enough to retain them, but Chumley had discovered one loose end. Once you discover a loose end of interlink wire you can unravel it as easily as knitting, and this was precisely what he had done. So Bert, who had also just been about to sit down to his Christmas dinner, set to work to repair the cage. Within an hour or so it was ready once more to receive the chimps. So finally, at four o'clock, we got the chimps back into their cage, and made our way to our various Christmas dinners. Catha, Sam, Jacquie and myself, sat down to charred turkey and vegetables that looked as though they had been trodden on by an exceptionally heavy elephant, but at least we had some wine on ice as compensation.

2. Just Jeremy

Dear Mr Durrell,

I am ten years old and in my opinion you are the best zoologist in the British Isles (except Peter Scott). Would you please send me your autograph?

The following year things looked much brighter and we had something concrete to show for our work. Catha worked like a beaver in order to keep the Trust and zoo accounts in order, and to control our overdraft, and also to control me, for I have a habit of over-spending without thinking.

'Wouldn't flamingoes be nice,' I would exclaim enthusiastically.

'Oh, yes, beautiful,' Catha would say. 'How much do they cost?'

'Oh, not very expensive,' I'd say. 'Somewhere in the neighbourhood of a hundred and twenty pounds each, I suppose.'

The happy smile would fade from Catha's face and a steely glint would come into her green eyes.

'Mr Durrell,' she would purr, 'do you know the size of our overdraft?'

'Oh, yes, yes,' I'd say hastily. 'It was only a suggestion.'

However, in spite of Catha's disinclination to part with any cash, we did make progress.

Aided by Jeremy and John Mallet we had completely re-organized the zoo. We worked out a card index of every animal in the place. Each animal had three cards: one pink, one blue, and one white. The white card was the history card and contained such details as where the specimen was obtained, its condition on arrival, and so on. The second card, the pink one, was the medical card and contained a full record of the animal's health and any veterinary treatment it had received. The blue card was the behaviour card, and probably the most important, for on it were noted such things as courtship displays, gestation periods, territory markings and a host of other things. We also instituted a large Day Book in Jeremy's office; a sort of diary to which every member of the staff had access so that they could note down anything of interest among their charges. These were then transferred to the appropriate cards. By this means we managed to start amassing some fascinating material. It is really astonishing how little is known about the average animal. I have a fairly comprehensive library of about a thousand books but you consult it for something quite simple, like, let us say, the courtship display of the creature in question, and you will find absolutely no mention of it anywhere.

The second thing we did was to adopt a new feeding system. I had read that Basle zoo had worked out a special formula which they fed, in addition to the normal food, to their animals, and which not only improved their condition but also their breeding potential. It had apparently been discovered that, however well you fed your animals — and we always gave ours the best that was obtainable — there were traces of minerals and various other substances which they did not obtain in their food and which were essential for their well-being. This form of 'cake' supplemented it. So I wrote to Dr Ernst Lang at Basle zoo and he very kindly sent me full details, and then we had a conference with Mr Le Marquand, the zoo's miller, and he made up the cake for us. It looked like a rather unattractive brown dough when it was finally completed, and we viewed it with some suspicion. However, I told Jeremy to give it a week's trial and see what would happen. At that time, Jeremy was frequently a visitor to the flat to consult me about various matters. There would be a knock on the front door, it would open, Jeremy's head would poke round, and he would say,

'Er, just Jeremy.'

And he would then come into the drawing-room where I would be working, to discuss whatever the problem of the day might be. After a week of trying the new food, there came the familiar rap on the front door and a voice said, 'Er, just Jeremy.'

'Come in, Jeremy,' I called.

He came and stood, wearing his worried expression, in the doorway of the drawing-room. Jeremy is tall, with hair the colour of ripe corn, a nose like the Duke of Wellington's, and very blue eyes which, when he is worried, are inclined to squint slightly. Now he was squinting, so there was obviously something the matter.

'What's the problem?' I inquired.

'Well, it's this new cake mixture,' he said. 'The – um – animals don't seem to like it. Some of the monkeys have eaten a little of it, I think more out of curiosity than anything else, but none of the other things is taking it.'

'How about the apes?' I inquired.

'No, they won't touch it at all,' said Jeremy gloomily. 'I've tried every way – even putting it in their milk – and they won't take it.'

'Have you tried starving them?' I inquired.

'No,' said Jeremy, looking a little guilty. 'I haven't, as a matter of fact.'

'Well, try it,' I suggested. 'Cut out all their food to-morrow, except their milk, and only give them the cake. See whether that will have any effect.'

The following day there came the familiar knock on the front door and the familiar, 'Er, just Jeremy.' Jeremy appeared once more at the drawing-room door.

'It's about the apes,' he said. 'We did starve them and gave them only the cake and milk. But they wouldn't eat the cake. So where do we go from here?'

I was as nonplussed as he was. This cake was fed to all the animals in Basle zoo and they ate it with every evidence of enjoyment. There was obviously something lacking in our cake to make it palatable. We phoned up Mr Le Marquand for his advice.

'What do you think we could put in it, to make it more attractive?' we asked.

He thought about the problem for some minutes, and then came up with a brilliant suggestion.

'What about aniseed?' he said. 'It's completely harmless, and it's a flavour that most animals seem to like.'

'Well,' I said, 'it can't do any harm. Will you make us up some with some aniseed in?'

'Yes,' he said, and forthwith produced a cake that had a strong smell of aniseed.

The moment this was introduced into the cages all the animals went wild about it. In fact, today, they take their cake in preference even to their favourite foods. In consequence, their condition has improved tremendously, and so have our breeding results. Within a year after the introduction of the cake into the diet, we had bred twelve species of mammals and ten species of bird and were feeling exceedingly proud of ourselves.

I think the birth that was of the greatest importance that year, and also caused us the most anxiety, was that of our South American tapir. Claudius, his father, I had collected while I was in Argentina, and he had, in his time, caused a considerable amount of trouble by escaping from the zoo grounds, eating up a friend's garden, ploughing through all the cloches in our nearest neighbour's farm, and many similar escapades. But now, since we'd found him a wife whom we called Claudette, he had settled down to be a staid and portly animal. Tapirs look not unlike brown, elongated, Shetland ponies, with long wiffly noses vaguely reminiscent of an elephant's trunk. They are benign and friendly beasts on the whole. As soon as Claudette had become old enough, mating had taken place and the various matings had been carefully noted on their behaviour card. It was then that we discovered how invaluable these cards were going to be, for as soon as Claudette showed signs of being pregnant, we could work back to the date of the last mating and thus judge reasonably accurately when she would be due to have her youngster.

One day there came the familiar tap on the front door, a voice said, 'Er, just Jeremy,' and Jeremy came in, wearing his worried look.

'It's about Claudette, Mr Durrell,' he began. 'I think she's due to give birth about September, according to the cards, and, er, I was wondering whether you thought it advisable to move her into the other paddock, away from Claudius?'

We discussed this at some length, and decided that perhaps it might be a wise manoeuvre to separate them, as we did not know what Claudius's reactions to a baby would be. In any case he was inclined to be short-sighted and might well trample on it accidentally. So Claudette was moved into the other paddock where she could still smell and rub noses with Claudius through the wire, but could give birth in safety. It was towards the time when we thought she should be almost ready that she started to cause us considerable anxiety. True, her girth had increased, but absolutely no movement could be felt from the baby and there was no sign of any milk in her udders. Jeremy, Tommy Begg, our veterinary surgeon, and I had a long conference.

'She's got such a damned thick skin,' said Tommy gloomily, 'and she's so tough otherwise, that I can't press my fingers in far enough to feel any movement from the baby at all.'

'Well, according to the cards,' said Jeremy, who by now was treating them as a sort of oracle, 'she should be having it any day now.'

'What worries me,' I said, 'is that she's got no milk. Surely she should have some milk by now?'

We all leant on the rail of the paddock and stared at Claudette, who gave the minute and ridiculous little squeak that tapirs give, and continued chewing meditatively on a hawthorn branch, completely oblivious of our worried faces.

'Well, if she does give birth,' said Tommy, 'and she's got no milk, you'll have to hand-rear the baby. What's the composition of tapir's milk?'

'I haven't a clue,' I said, 'but I can look it up in the library.'

We all trooped down to my study, but in not a single book could we find the composition of tapir's milk.

'Well,' said Tommy, after the forty-seventh book had been read and found wanting, 'we'll just have to take a risk on it and make up a composition as near to mare's milk as possible. I should think that would do.'

Feeding bottles and teats were got ready and sterilized, and all the ingredients for making up something similar to mare's milk put ready to hand. We waited and waited, and Claudette showed not the slightest sign of giving birth. Then, one day, her hut was cleaned out as normal at about ten-thirty in the morning. There was still no sign of the baby, but at three o'clock that afternoon Geoff, who was looking after her, came tearing down the back drive, his face glowing with excitement.

'She's had it! She's had it!' he shouted.

Jeremy and I, who had been standing there in grave discussion over some other matter, immediately rushed up the back slope and into Claudette's paddock. She was outside, chewing on a large bowl of carrots and mixed fruit, and took absolutely no notice of our intrusion. We peered cautiously into the hut and there, in the straw, was one of the most adorable baby animals I've ever seen. It was about the size of a small dog and striped, as all baby tapirs are, with vivid white stripes that ran the length of its body on its chocolate-brown fur, making it look like some sort of animated humbug. It seemed to me amazing that such a large baby could have been inside Claudette and yet we had been unable to feel any movement whatsoever. He

must have been born within the hour, for his fur was still damp in patches where Claudette had licked him. We helped him gingerly to his feet so that we could sex him, and he waddled about the hut for a few moments before lying down again. He looked, with his white stripes, extraordinarily conspicuous on the straw, but when you translated this pattern into terms of light filtering through the thick forest canopy overhead in the places where tapirs lived, you could see that it was the most perfect camouflage.

We immediately christened him Caesar, to carry on the Roman line, as it were, and then went to see whether Claudette had any milk. This was the most worrying thing of all, for hand-rearing baby animals at the best of times is not easy. To our immense surprise we found that, between ten o'clock in the morning and three o'clock in the afternoon, her udders had filled completely with milk and she had a plentiful supply. That was a great worry off our shoulders. She proved an exemplary mother and it wasn't long before Caesar was trotting round the paddock at her heels. Another interesting thing we noticed was that she would feed him while lying down, and he would lie down beside her, sucking vigorously at her teats.

Now, as I said before, my library is fairly extensive and tapirs have been bred in zoological gardens for a great number of years; yet nowhere had we found these three facts recorded. First, that it is almost impossible to tell whether the female is pregnant or not, that is to say that you cannot feel the baby kicking inside her. Second, that her teats only fill with milk when the baby has been born. Third, that she suckles the young while lying down. Also, since Claudette was a very amiable beast, it was easy for us to obtain a sample of milk from her and send it for a break-down to the Public Analyst. This meant that if, in the future, we had a female tapir give birth to a youngster and she did not have any milk to feed it, we would know the exact composition necessary. All these items were duly noted on the cards, and eventually published in our Annual Report.

Another interesting birth that took place at roughly the same time was that of a Gelada baboon. The adult Gelada baboon is a handsome creature with a great shawl of chocolate-coloured fur, and an extraordinary, almost heart-shaped, patch of bright red skin on the chest that makes it look as though the fur has been scraped away leaving only raw skin underneath. Algie was the male, and he was a great character. His hind legs were slightly too short and bowed, which gave him the most curious, pansy walk. He would always greet you, when you went to the cage, by waddling up to the wire, turning his upper lip right back so that you could see his gums and his huge teeth, and uttering little moaning cries of delight as you talked to him. He shared his quarters, to begin with, with a South African baboon, but it wasn't long before we got him a mate, whom we decided to call Amber, for, as a member of the staff remarked, Algie was forever at Amber. Algie lived for his food and his womenfolk, so it was not unduly surprising that, in a very short space of time, Amber became pregnant.

Baboons of all species in the wild state have an interesting social structure, so we left the South African baboon in with the two Geladas to see how this would work out when the baby was eventually born. Algie, who was the dominant animal in the cage, distributed his favours equally between his own mate and this totally un-related African baboon. Next in line of authority was the baboon herself, and Amber, prior to the birth of the baby, was the most lowly member of the troop. The principal reason we left the African baboon in with them was that, if we had removed her, the chain of authority would have been altered and Algie and his mate would have started the usual bullying and bickering that goes on between any pair of primates. As it was, Algie bullied the South African baboon and she, in turn, bullied Amber, but in a much more gentle fashion than Algie would have done. There was a risk that if we left the South African baboon in the cage, since she was the dominant animal over Amber, she might

damage or even eat the youngster when it was born. However, we decided to take the risk.

In the wild state the majority of baboons have worked
out a very complex social system which has only recently
been investigated to any great extent. It has been observed
that, when a female baboon gives birth to a baby, there is
great excitement amongst all the females of the troop, particularly the elderly females who are past child-bearing.
To begin with they gather round the mother and examine
the baby with great interest, although not being allowed
to touch it. Gradually, the mother ceases to guard it quite
so jealously and then the older females vie with each other
in taking turns to hold the baby, grooming it and carrying
it about with them. In this particular instance, if all three
animals had been of the same species, one could have
assumed that the same process would have been observed.
However there was some doubt as to whether the older
South African baboon would react in this way to the baby
of a completely different species.

The great day came. The baby was born sometime during
the night in the baboons' bedroom. It was observed at
eight o'clock the following morning, perfectly clean and
dry. It was clinging tenaciously to its mother and there
was no sign of an umbilical cord or afterbirth. When they
were let out into their outside cage it became immediately
obvious that the South African baboon was as excited and,
one might almost say, delighted with the birth of the
baby as the mother. She sat as close to Amber as possible,
generally facing her and occasionally putting her arms round
her protectively, so that the baby, who was clinging on
to the front of its mother, was wedged between the two of
them. Algie, who, as I said, had hitherto been the dominant
animal in the cage, was intrigued by the infant and
obviously wanted to examine it, but whenever he approached Amber she would round on him, turning back

her upper lips, chattering her teeth and uttering a 'yahhr-ring' noise which we had not previously heard in her vocabulary. This had the effect of making him retreat, so that all he could do was circle the pair of females and the baby, keeping about two yards away, and peering hopefully to see if he could catch a glimpse of it.

This state of affairs lasted about twenty-four hours, then he was allowed closer so that he could groom his mate and the South African baboon. Five days after the birth they had reverted more or less to their normal behaviour. The South African baboon still acted in a protective way to both mother and baby but Algie was allowed to embrace and groom his wife. He was not, as far as was observed, allowed to touch the baby at all. The baby was extremely strong and healthy and, in contrast with most other baby baboons, had only a slightly wrinkled face. Within twenty-four hours its eyes could see and focus with great accuracy, and it would follow the movement of your hand or body some six feet away outside the cage. On the fifth day the mother allowed it to climb down and walk a little way on the floor, though she kept it within arms' reach the whole time. After seven days, however, this happy state of affairs came to an end, for the South African baboon, who was now allowed to hold the baby, became too possessive and would hold on to it even when it was obvious that the baby wanted to go back to its mother to be fed. We were forced to remove the South African baboon and Algie into a separate cage so that the youngster could thrive.

The Trust was now coming up to its first birthday, and we felt we ought to have some sort of celebration. We decided to have a Members' Day, vulgarly known to us as 'The Bun Fight'. We would close the zoo for the day except to members, invite various celebrities over and have a lunch which we hoped would be attended by the Gov-

ernor of the island and the Bailiff. In the evening there
would be a fund-raising dinner at which we hoped our
celebrities would give speeches pleading our cause. The
amount of work which went into this was considerable.
There were hotels to be booked, menus to be worked out,
seating plans which drove us nearly mad, and various
other things. It was also the time of the year when fog
is prevalent in Jersey, and if there was any fog anywhere
near Jersey it inevitably settled with unerring accuracy on

the airport. It was therefore imperative that we should get all our celebrities over at least a day before, otherwise we might find ourselves with nobody to entertain. Ninety per cent of this work was done by Catha and she did it magnificently, but I could see that it would be necessary in the future not only to have a Council but also several subcommittees to take care of such projects.

One of the committees I decided to form was a fundraising committee, and I was brooding on this one day when I went down to meet Jacquie at the airport. As I entered the arrivals hall, my mind occupied with other matters, I suddenly found myself face to face with one of the loveliest girls I had seen in my life. She had black hair, very large hazel-green eyes, and was wearing an expression of such melting love and kindness that I felt sure it could not be directed at me. However, she came closer and I discovered that it was. My spirits rose. Perhaps, after all, the slight pot I was developing and the bags under my eyes were not as noticeable as I had thought, or maybe there were even some girls that liked them. Then my spirits fell again, for I saw she was carrying a collection box.

'Would you,' she said, in tones like melting honey, 'would you like to contribute?'

'Certainly,' I said. 'How could I resist eyes like that, anyway?'

I fumbled in my pocket and quite by mistake pushed a ten shilling note into her box instead of the half-crown I had intended.

'I bet with a face like yours you are doing a roaring trade,' I said.

She smiled sweetly.

'Oh, I'm not doing too badly,' she said.

'Well, you should try collecting for us sometime.'

'Why don't you ask me?'

'Maybe I will,' I said, and then the Tannoy announced the arrival of Jacquie's plane and I went to the entrance doors. It was while I was standing there that a brilliant thought occurred to me. There was the very girl, and she had actually offered her services. She would be perfect for fund-raising. Nobody could resist those eyes, I felt sure. I waited impatiently for Jacquie to arrive, grabbed her by the arm and unceremoniously dragged her back into the arrivals hall.

'Hurry up. Hurry up,' I said. 'I'm looking for a girl.'

'Not again,' said Jacquie.

'No, no. This is a very special, very beautiful girl. She was here a minute ago, collecting something for something.'

'What on earth do you want her for?' asked Jacquie, suspiciously.

'Well, she's perfect for the fund-raising committee,' I said. 'And she actually offered, and like a fool I didn't get her name.'

I looked frantically round the hall, but it was completely devoid of anything except elderly dowager duchesses and retired colonels.

'Damn!' I said. 'I've missed the opportunity of a lifetime.'

'Well, surely you can find out who she is? She must be somebody local,' said Jacquie.

'I don't know,' I said. 'I suppose I could ask Hope.'

As soon as we got home I phoned up Hope.

'Hope,' I said, 'who is a very beautiful girl, with hazel-green eyes and dark hair, who was collecting for something or other at the airport today?'

'Really, Gerry!' said Hope. 'You do ask the most impossible questions. How do you expect *me* to know? And, if it comes to that, what do you want to know for?'

'I want to start a fund-raising committee,' I said, 'and she seemed to me to be an absolutely ideal person to have on it.'

Hope chuckled.

'Well, I can't think of anybody off-hand,' she said. 'You might, of course, try Lady Calthorpe. She's supposed to be very good at fund-raising.'

I groaned. I could just imagine what Lady Calthorpe was like. Long yellow teeth, cropped iron-grey hair, tweeds smelling of spaniels, and spaniels smelling of tweeds.

'Well, I'll think about it,' I said.

So the day of the bun fight dawned and, needless to say, there was fog at the airport. Pandemonium reigned about getting Peter Scott and his wife over, and we only did it in the nick of time, with the aid of somebody's private plane. However, everything went off smoothly. In the morning I took Peter and his wife round the zoo, introduced them to members of the staff, and explained the work that we were trying to do. Peter, to my delight, seemed very impressed.

The lunch was a very pleasant occasion; principally, I think, because nobody made any speeches. Then, in the afternoon, we all went round the zoo once more. There was just time for a bath and change before setting out for the real event of the day, which was the fund-raising dinner. To this we had invited a small, but select, gathering of people, some of whom we hoped might be able to help us in other ways. Lord Jersey was the first speaker and he then introduced Peter Scott, who gave a marvellous speech on various aspects of conservation and the importance of the work that we were trying to do. I was supposed to be the next speaker, and was shuffling my notes in a desultory fashion in preparation, when my gaze was suddenly riveted on a girl sitting some distance away at another part of the table. It was the one that I had seen at the airport.

What on earth, I thought, was she doing here? The problem so intrigued me that I almost forgot my speech. However, I struggled through it and sat down. I was determined, at the first available opportunity, to make my way across the room and capture the girl before she could escape for the second time.

Soon there came a general shuffling of chairs and people started to leave the tables. I made my way, with all the speed that politeness would permit, through the mass of distinguished friends, and managed to catch the girl just as she was going out of the door. I laid my hand upon her shoulder, rather in the manner of a store detective who is arresting a shop-lifter. She turned and raised disdainful eyebrows at me.

'You're the girl I met at the airport,' I said.

'Yes,' she said. 'That's why I'm here.'

'Well, at the airport,' I continued, 'you said that you would be willing to help us raise money. Was that just a joke, or do you still mean it?'

'Of course I mean it.'

For once in my life I had a piece of paper and a pen in my pocket.

'Could I have your name and telephone number, and could I get in touch with you and discuss this further?' I asked.

'But of course,' she said, 'any time you like.'

'Um . . . your name?'

'Saranne Calthorpe.'

I was flabbergasted. I stared at her for a moment.

'But . . . but you can't be *Lady* Calthorpe,' I said, rather petulantly.

'Well, I have been for quite a number of years.'

'But . . . I mean . . . where's the cropped hair, and the spaniels, and the look of an ancient mare?' I asked in desperation.

'Do I look like an ancient mare?' she inquired with interest.

'No, no!' I said. '. . . I didn't mean that. What I meant was that I *thought* you'd look like an ancient mare. Are you sure there're not two Lady Calthorpes on the island?'

'As far as I know,' she said, with supreme dignity, 'I am the only one. You can phone me any time you like,' she added, and gave me her address and telephone number.

I went back to Jacquie, jubilant.

'I've found the girl,' I said.

'Which particular one?' inquired Jacquie.

'The one I was telling you about,' I said, impatiently. 'The one at the airport. She's Lady Calthorpe.'

'But I thought you said that Lady Calthorpe was surrounded by spaniels and tweeds and things,' said Jacquie.

'No, no, no! This is that . . . that . . . lovely creature in . . . in . . . a black sort of dress with white jobs on it,' I said.

'Oh, that one,' said Jacquie. 'Yes . . . well, I suppose she could raise money.'

'I shall contact her instantly,' I said, 'tomorrow morning. But now, for God's sake, let's go home and go to bed.'

And so we did.

Taken all round the bun fight had been a great success. We'd had a chance to get advice from people like James Fisher, Walter van den Berg, the Director of Antwerp zoo, Richard Fitter of the Fauna Preservation Society, and many other people who had not only seen fit to praise the work we were doing, but gave constructive criticism. Not only that, but at last the amount of money raised would enable us to start work on our most urgent project, a series of new, large, outdoor cages for our apes. The plans for these had long been mouldering on the drawing-board, while Jeremy and I gloated over them. They were going to cost far more money than the Trust could afford. But after the bun fight we knew that we could start to build them and we were jubilant at the thought.

Now, it has always been my contention that the two most dangerous creatures to let loose unsupervised in a zoo are a veterinary surgeon and an architect. The vet will insist on treating wild animals as if they are domestic ones. A bush dog or a dingo may be of the dog family, but you cannot treat them as though they were pekinese or spaniels. Generally, the vet, in despair, says: 'Well, I should put it down, if I were you.' We were fortunate in having two vets, Mr Blampied and Mr Begg, who took the opposite view. The last thing they ever wanted to do was to put any animal down at all.

Architects are a different kettle of fish. If left unsupervised, they will design you a cage that is a poem architecturally but useless from the point of view of the staff who have to use it or, more to the point, the animals who have to live in it. When it had come to the cages for the apes, Jeremy and I had watched the designs with great care to make sure that no mistakes were made. They were extremely difficult cages to design because they had to be built on sloping ground, facing south, along the wall of the mammal house. But the ground sloped in three different directions, which meant we had to build up a great staging of concrete upon which the cages could stand. The final design that Bill Davis, our architect, produced for us pleased me very much. Each cage was almost triangular so that the inmates of any cage could see what was going on in the other two. Apes are just as inquisitive about what their neighbours are doing as any human beings, so instead of muslin curtains from behind which they could peep, we gave them bars. The roof of this construction was sloping slightly backwards so that the apes could get the maximum amount of sunshine.

The firm which was to build the cages moved in and began to clear the site. The cages in which the apes were living at the time were inside the house but they each had a window from which they could see the construction work going on, and this fascinated them. Oscar the orang-utan, who is the most mechanically-minded of all the apes, would sit, almost literally all day, with his face pressed against the glass, watching the cement being mixed and laid, an absorbed expression on his rather Chinese face. I went down one morning to see how the work was progressing, and was talking to one of the men.

'I see that Oscar is making sure you build the cages properly,' I said, pointing to where the ape was sitting with his face pressed against the glass.

''im!' said the man. ''onestly, 'e sits there all day long. It's worse than 'aving a bloody foreman watching you!'

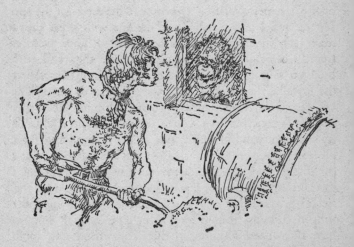

3. A Lion in Labour

Dear Mr Durrell,

My name is Miriam. I have written to ask your advice on the following:

1. *Would it be at all possible for me to get a baby lion?*
2. *If so where would I get it and do you know about what the cost would be?*
3. *How old is the youngest I could get it (take it from its mother)?*
4. *Where would I have to keep it?*
5. *How old would I be able to keep?*
6. *What would I feed a very small, baby lion?*
7. *How large would he actually be?*

And anything else you think I would need to know!

Thank you very much . . .

In any large collection of wild animals you are liable to have your crop of illness and accidents, and sometimes these prove fatal, for animals are no less mortal than man. Under the heading 'accidents' you have, I'm afraid, to include the behaviour of the average member of the public. We have had, in the past, instances of monkeys being given razor blades and the great apes lighted pipes and cigarettes, so that they burnt themselves. Unless you have somebody permanently on watch it is difficult to guard against this sort of behaviour.

Take, for example, the case of our two macaws, Captain Koe and McCoy. Now these were colourful birds and of a benign disposition, so when the weather was fine we

would take them out of their cage and put them on a low granite wall that ran along the side of the mammal house where they would sit in the sunshine, preen their brilliant feathers and exchange hoarse chuckling conversation with any visitor who happened to be passing. One day, an exceptionally large lady, presumably exhausted by her tour of the zoo, went to rest on the wall where Captain Koe was sitting. Believe it or not, she actually sat on top of him. That anyone could sit on a bird the size of a macaw, with such multi-coloured brilliant feathering, may seem incredible. It is a great pity that Captain Koe couldn't

have retaliated by biting the lady in question for there was ample target for him to aim at and macaws' beaks are among the biggest of the parrot family. However, he was simply squashed.

Our maintenance man, who happened to be passing

at the time, noted the incident. The woman herself seemed completely unaware of the fact that she had done anything unusual. The maintenance man picked up the bird and brought it immediately to the office. Luckily, at that precise moment we had Tommy Begg, our veterinary surgeon, in the zoo doing his weekly check-up on the animals, and he immediately attended to Captain Koe. Both legs had been broken and these Tommy splinted skilfully, but in addition to this the ribs and breast-bone had been crushed and some of the ribs had pierced the lung. So, in spite of all we could do, in a short time the macaw was dead.

The thing which amazed me most was the woman's behaviour. Even allowing for the fact that she was short-sighted and couldn't see a large bird clad in brilliant scarlet and blue feathering sitting on a wall, after she had sat on it she must have known that she had done some damage. Not only did she not come to the office to explain her mistake and inquire after the bird's condition, but she did not even bother to phone up and find out how the bird was getting on. This is only one instance of the attitude of the general public. I should think, on average, one spends about seventy per cent of one's time protecting the animals from the public rather than the other way round.

Like any sensible zoo, we do not allow the public to feed the animals. This is because they might give them the wrong sort of food, or too much of something that they happen to like particularly, and this will prevent them from eating the carefully balanced diet we have worked out for them. For instance, the great apes will go on eating chocolate, rather like children, until they feel sick, and then they will refuse their evening meal which would have done them much more good. They may then perhaps develop stomach trouble, and you have a long job curing the complaint that has arisen from wrong feeding. But some of the public who come to the zoo don't take the slightest notice of the signs that we have all over the place, saying 'Please do not feed these animals', and continue to hurl bars of chocolate and other tidbits with gay abandon through the bars of the cages. One has, in any sizeable collection of animals, enough veterinary work to do during the course of the year without it being added to by the stupidity, and sometimes the cruelty, of the visitors.

At one end of the zoo grounds we have a small lake, and here we kept a mixed collection of water fowl, including some quite rare species. They had lived there happily and bred for quite a number of years. Then we had a particularly hot summer. The little stream that fed the lake died away to a mere trickle and the lake itself became more and more shallow. Soon we started finding the odd dead bird which, after post mortem, gave no satisfactory answers as to why it had died. And then, suddenly, we had a crop of about six birds die all at once, including two of our rare specimens. Tommy Begg viewed with mystification the dismal row of corpses that awaited him on his Monday morning visit.

'What the hell's the matter with that lake?' he demanded, irritably. 'We've had the water tested, and there's nothing wrong with these birds as far as I can see.'

Then he had an idea.

'The only thing I haven't looked for is gizzard worm,' he said. 'I wonder if it could be that?'

Seizing the nearest body, which happened to be that of a Spur-winged goose, he carefully slit the gizzard with his scalpel. There was nothing to be seen. Then he opened the crop of the bird, and found the solution to the mystery. For the crop contained approximately an egg-cupful of twelve-bore lead pellets. Examining the crops of the other dead birds we found an equal quantity of lead shot in each one, and in one of them we even found the metal end of a twelve-bore shotgun cartridge. Now the crop of a bird can really be described as its teeth, in the sense that most birds take a certain quantity of sand or gravel or even small pebbles with their food. These lodge in the crop and help to grind and masticate the food as it passes through. As the sand or gravel or small stones are worn away over a period, the bird picks up a fresh supply to replenish its 'teeth'. These birds had, from somewhere or other, found a large supply of lead pellets and had naturally eaten them, presumably mistaking them for small pebbles or gravel. They certainly acted as teeth in the crop, but the food was wearing them away and the birds were suffering from lead poisoning.

Of course, as soon as we realized the mysterious cause of these deaths, we caught up all the birds on the lake and searched the shore line carefully to see if we could find the source of the pellets. As there were so many of them in the crops of the birds that had died, we felt sure that they must have come across a whole boxful of twelve-bore cartridges, or something similar, but though we searched hard we could not find the spot where the birds had found them. One of the birds that we had removed from the lake started to sicken. It was obviously suffering from lead poisoning, so we tried to save it by the use of calcium disodium versenate injected intravenously. Unfortunately this failed and the bird died. How such a quantity of lead shot could be found in the lake remained a mystery for some time, until we discovered that until after the war the lake had not been a lake at all. It had just been a small valley with a tiny stream running through it. The owner of the property, our present landlord, Major Fraser, had dammed it up and turned it into a small lake. We came to the conclusion that, during the German occupation of the island, somebody had been in possession of a quantity of twelve-bore cartridges and, afraid of being found with them, had buried them in the valley. The gradual action of water and mud had worn away the cardboard cases of the cartridges and had released the pellets in a heap into the water, and during the exceptionally hot summer the water level had dropped, thus allowing the ducks and geese access to areas of mud which they would not otherwise have been able to reach.

There are, of course, a number of other things that happen in the zoo against which you are completely powerless to protect yourself. For example, our African civets gave birth to a litter of cubs. This was quite an event as not many zoos had managed to breed civets. For three days the female proved an exemplary mother and then, for

some reason unknown to us, she turned on her cubs and ate them. Then there was the case of our Serval cats. These handsome, long-legged cats, with their pricked ears, short tails and coats a lovely orangey-brown heavily spotted with black, are very beautiful creatures indeed, and we were extremely pleased when Tammy had two kittens. She too proved to be an excellent mother and for about a week the kittens throve and suckled well and she seemed very contented. And then, one day, on looking into her den, we discovered both cubs dead. Why this should have happened we had no idea. The cubs were completely unmarked so they obviously hadn't been bitten by her. But a post mortem soon revealed what the trouble was. They had died of suffocation. Tammy, during the night presumably, had rolled over, lain on top of the cubs, and suffocated them both without realizing it. This sometimes happens to

domestic cats, with their first litter of babies, until they've learnt the arts of motherhood.

But I think probably our most complicated veterinary problem occurred when our lioness, Sheba, became pregnant. Everything seemed to be going fine, and she was getting near her time. I had to go into town one day to lunch with some friends and, as I always do when I leave the zoo, I left the address and the telephone number of the restaurant, so that should there be any emergency they could get in touch with me immediately. I had no sooner finished lunch than I got a telephone call to say that Sheba had started to give birth, but that she had got one youngster half out and half in and, strain though she would, she didn't seem able to pass it. The cub was obviously dead. I grabbed a taxi, got back to the zoo as quickly as I could, and Jeremy and I reviewed the situation. She had been straining then for two or two and a half hours and, as I said, the cub was limp and dangling and obviously dead, but she was unable to dislodge it and seemed in great distress.

'What we ought to do,' said Jeremy, 'is get her into a small cage. Then perhaps we could help her in some way.'

Unfortunately the den was rather a large one and in order to get her into a smaller cage we would have had to go in with her and drive her. This was a risk I was not prepared to take. I had an idea. I knew that the London Zoo possessed a Capchur gun. This is like a revolver except that it shoots a dart which acts like a hypodermic syringe, penetrating the animal's flank or whatever part of the body you are aiming at, and giving it an injection which can be an anaesthetic, an antibiotic or something similar. I thought that if I phoned London Zoo there was a chance that they would fly it over to me so that we could use it on Sheba. I went into the house and put in a call to London Zoo.

Needless to say, this was a Saturday. All crises like this seem to happen on a Saturday. When I eventually got through to London Zoo sanitorium they said, yes, indeed, they had a Capchur gun, but that the only person allowed to use it was their chief veterinary officer, Dr Oliver Graham Jones. The police were very strict about it and would not allow it off the premises. Well, I'd known Oliver Graham Jones for a number of years, and I knew that he would bend the law a little if he could. I asked if I could speak to him. They were terribly sorry, they said, but he was at home for the weekend. Well, could they get me his private number? Yes, they could, and they did, and in due course I got Oliver on the telephone. I explained the situation to him and he was most sympathetic.

'But, my dear boy,' he said, 'the first thing is, I can't send the thing over without police permission, and, secondly, unless you've used one of these before they can be extremely dangerous. Unless you get the right charge in the gun, the syringe that it propels, instead of acting purely as a hypodermic, acts more like a rifle bullet and you're liable to kill your animal rather than cure it. They're tricky things to handle.'

'Well, there's nothing for it, then,' I said. 'We'll have to try and drive her into a small crate. That'll mean going in, I suppose, with flaming torches.'

'Good heavens!' said Oliver, shocked to the core. 'You can't do that! You might all be killed – especially when she's in that condition. She's not going to take kindly to that sort of treatment.'

'Well, there's nothing else to do, is there?'

Oliver thought for some moments.

'How long,' he said, 'would it take me to get over to Jersey?'

'It depends on the flights,' I said, 'but, possibly, about an hour.'

'Well, if you can get me a flight I'll go to the zoo, get the gun, and come over and do the job for you.'

'That's marvellous,' I said, enthusiastically. 'I'll get on to our travel agent right away and ring you back.'

Now to add to the complications it was the height of the holiday season and practically every plane was booked by honeymooners or families coming to spend their holidays in Jersey. I got on to our friendly travel agents and explained the situation to them. Could they possibly get me a seat from Heathrow to Jersey on a flight as soon as possible? They said they would ring me back; so for half an hour I paced the room, metaphorically chewing my fingernails. Then the phone rang. It was the travel agents: there was just one seat on a Heathrow flight, leaving at about five-thirty. I told them to phone Heathrow and warn them to expect Dr Oliver Graham Jones. I then phoned Oliver back and told him.

'Good lord,' he said, 'that doesn't give me very much time. Anyway, I'll do the best I can.'

'I'll be at the airport to meet you.'

'Right,' he said. 'I only hope to God I don't get caught in a traffic jam.'

I was at the plane to meet him, and hurried him to the car. Oliver has dark hair and large brown eyes and looks as though he is a successful Harley Street specialist rather than a veterinary surgeon. As we drove to the zoo I told him what had happened so far. The cub was still half-way out, and Sheba was still straining and obviously in great distress. I'd alerted our own two veterinary surgeons, and they had brought up the necessary apparatus because, as Oliver had told me on the phone, we might have to do a ceasarean operation to save her life. When we got to the zoo, our veterinary surgeons were there with all the necessary apparatus. A table had been hurriedly put in the outside of the lion cage and floodlights were rigged up over it. It made a very rough operating theatre but it was the best we could do in the time. Then Oliver had a look at his patient who, exhausted by straining, was lying down in one corner. She snarled rather pathetically at us.

'Yes,' said Oliver. 'We haven't got much time. It's a jolly good thing I managed to catch that plane.'

He carefully unpacked the Capchur gun which he had brought with him and loaded the syringe with the necessary anaesthetic. Then, taking careful aim, he fired at Sheba. There was a dull 'phlunk' as the dart hit her flank. She gave a small jump and glanced down, but apart from this took no notice at all. Presently, as the dart started to take effect, she got to her feet and staggered a few steps about the den, then lay down again. We got a long pole and prodded her gently. There was no response, so we knew that she must be unconscious. Then we went round to the other side of the den and lifted the sliding door in order to drag her out. I wanted to go in first to rope her legs, but Oliver wouldn't hear of it. He explained that some-times in the case of these anaesthetics, although the animal gave all the appearance of being unconscious, it could come round for just a brief enough second to make a nasty mess of you. So he went in first and I followed him. He put a bar of wood in her mouth and tied her muzzle securely round it. This not only helped to keep her mouth open so that she could breathe properly, but also prevented her from biting us should she regain consciousness. We then roped her feet and proceeded to haul her out. She was a tremendous weight and it took six of us to lift her on to the table. Polite as a professional Harley Street specialist, Oliver asked Mr Blampied and Mr Begg if they would like to perform the operation. They, equally politely, said that as he had been kind enough to come so far they thought the honour should go to him. The first thing to be done was to remove the cub. This was a fairly simple process. On examination, it proved to be most peculiar. It was almost as though somebody had put a bicycle pump beneath the skin and had pumped it full of air. Its bones were all flabby and soft, and its face was misshapen because of this gas-forming material inside the skin.

The next thing was carefully to shave the area on the side of her stomach where the incision had to be made. This was done with an electric hair-clipper which Mr Blampied had brought with him for the purpose. The area having been shaved, and Oliver having washed his hands and disinfected them, he was ready to start the operation. It was now fairly late and getting darkish, so we turned on the spotlights that we had arranged above the table. Their glare revealed that, outside the wire of the lion cage, were congregated the entire staff, all determined to watch the operation. I asked Oliver if he would mind if they came inside the cage so that they could get a closer look at what was going on, and Oliver said he would be delighted. So the staff trooped in and formed a semi-circle round the table, and Oliver, as he operated, gave a running commentary on what he was doing.

First he made a longitudinal slit along her side. As soon as he had actually penetrated the stomach itself, it deflated with a hissing noise and the most disgusting stench I have ever smelt in my life poured out. Oliver's hands moved rapidly and deftly. He enlarged the incision, seeming totally unaware of the stench which had sent one or two members of the staff slightly white, and then carefully dipped his hands into the lioness's stomach and, one by one, removed two more cubs. They were in exactly the same bloated, blown-up condition as the first one. All three cubs were placed in a bucket for future examination to try to ascertain exactly what the trouble was. Then Oliver had to remove the afterbirth, wash out the interior and sew up the stomach and the skin over it. This was covered with a thick layer of antibiotic powder, and she was injected with penicillin and streptomycin as an additional precaution. At this stage her breathing was shallow but regular. Throughout the operation she had been kept under an ordinary anaesthetic, that is to say with a mask over her mouth and nose, under the control of Mrs Blampied.

We slid her carefully off the table on to an improvised stretcher, carried her down and put her in a cage which had been specially prepared for her and which was big enough to allow her to stand up but not to move around, for the one fear was that she would try to get up too quickly and burst her stitches. The important thing was to keep her warm so that she didn't develop pneumonia, and so she was covered with blankets and hot water bottles were put all round her. Her tongue and mouth which, with the anaesthetic, had naturally grown very dry, had to be moistened with glucose and water at frequent intervals. This meant that Geoff, who was looking after the lions at the time, had to stay up all night replenishing the hot water bottles and keeping her tongue and mouth moist. At one point in the middle of the night, when he thought that she wasn't warm enough and couldn't find anything more suitable, he even went and took the eiderdown off his own bed to put over her. The following morning, recovery seemed to be progressing quite normally. We could get a reflex from her eye and she was obviously semi-conscious, but not conscious enough to be able to do anything really serious in the way of attacking us.

The swab, taken from her stomach, was examined at Leeds University, and a very unusual form of gas-forming organism, *Clostridium sordellii,* was isolated. Apparently, this organism can be picked up from the earth and is reasonably common in cattle, but hitherto hadn't been found in any member of the cat family.

After the operation had been completed, I had taken our troop of veterinary surgeons up to the flat for a drink, before driving Oliver to his hotel.

'Tell me,' he said to me, 'how many of your staff were present during the operation?'

'All of them,' I said. 'Including the ones that were on day off.'

'Good lord,' said Oliver. 'I wish I had such enthusiasm in London. I doubt if anybody would have turned up if I had been doing an operation like that. And yet you got all your staff to come.'

'I didn't *get* them to come,' I said. 'They came of their own accord.'

'Remarkable,' said Oliver. 'Try and keep them like that, won't you?'

'That's exactly what I intend to do,' I said.

And I hope that is what I have done.

When Sheba had fully recovered we decided to keep her separated from Leo for at least six months, because we did not want her to become pregnant again too quickly after so serious an operation. When they were eventually put back together they were very pleased to see each other and

in next to no time Sheba was pregnant again. Of course, we watched her with the greatest anxiety, but by this time I had sent to America and managed to obtain a Capchur gun of our own, so we felt that, should anything go wrong, we at least wouldn't have to drag Oliver over from London Zoo. Sheba gave birth to two fat, healthy cubs, without any difficulty whatsoever, and we all heaved a heartfelt sigh of relief. But her drama was not yet over. Once the cubs were big enough to be taken away from the mother, Sheba became pregnant once more.

As she had just given birth to two cubs quite normally, we felt sure that this next pregnancy would be the same. But when she was ready to have the cubs she picked up the gas-forming organism again, and once more we had to go through the same performance. With the Capchur gun we anaesthetized her, and then Mr Blampied and Tommy Begg did a caesarean and removed two cubs, both with the same extraordinary blown-up look about them as the first ones had had. Sheba was stitched up, given the usual injections of penicillin and so on, and moved once more into the cage that she had occupied for so long. Everything seemed to be progressing satisfactorily and then, one day, to our horror, she did the one thing that we hoped she would not do and could not guard against. Although the cage was long and narrow it did allow her to stand up and move about slightly. She must have stood up during the night to try and turn round, and in consequence had burst all her stitches.

Once more she had to be knocked out and the wound re-stitched. This was an extremely difficult job, for when the original stitches had burst, they had torn away all the flesh along the edge of the wound, and so, in order to close the gap, one now had to do huge stitches, some four or five inches in width, in order to find sufficient firm skin and flesh to stitch through. When this was over she was given the usual antibiotics and put back in her cage. The following morning she had recovered sufficiently to be able to raise her head and drink a little glucose and water. She was given a further penicillin injection and an Ionalyte drip was set up. But at midday her breathing seemed peculiar and, despite the administration of a heart stimulant, Sheba died. We were, of course, bitterly disappointed, but we felt we had done everything we could to try to save her. This third operation had been just too much for her strength to cope with.

4. Mr and Mrs D.

Dear Mr Durrell,
The other day a woodpecker flew into my hall and started to peck a hole in my grandfather clock. Is this an unusual occurrence?

It was, I think, Edgar Wallace who said that if a man had one nickname he was held in some esteem, but if he had two or more he was disliked. As far as I know, Jacquie and I have only one nickname in the zoo, if you can call it that; we are referred to by all the staff as Mr and Mrs D. This, I think, was started by Shep Mallet.

Shep, with his curly hair, blue eyes and wide ingratiating grin, is without doubt the most handsome male member of the staff. He has, in his time, broken more hearts than I care to remember, and practically every girl who has worked in the bird section has succumbed to his charms. In fact, I remember one girl being so deeply in love with him that she went to tell Jeremy that she could no longer bear to work in the zoo unless Shep returned her affections. As this was impossible she felt she would have to leave. As she was in the middle of telling Jeremy this, she suddenly wailed, 'Oh, Mr Mallinson, I love him so much I think I'm going to be sick!', rushed out of Jeremy's office and was sick, promptly, in the corridor. Since Shep's second name is Juan I've often wondered why we never christened him Don Juan, but Shep he became and Shep he remains, and he has all our quite large bird collection in his care.

Birds, on the whole, don't seem to display the same amount of character as animals do, but we have, at one time and another, had a great number of birds with very distinct personalities of their own. I think, perhaps, the best example of this was Trumpy, the Grey-winged Trumpeter from South America. Grey-winged Trumpeters are birds about the size of a hen with a high domed forehead that indicates great intellect, and large liquid eyes. Trumpy, being quite tame, was allowed the run of the zoo, and one of the things he used to do was to settle in any new arrivals. That is to say, he would go and stand near or, preferably, in the cage of any new arrival for twenty-four hours until he felt it had settled down, and then he would move on somewhere else.

He took to flying over the fence and bullying the two penguins we had at that time. They stood this as long as they could and then one day they rounded on him and one of them, with a lucky swipe, knocked him into their pond. Trumpy, of course, was not a water bird and so the penguins had him at their mercy. We found him floating on the surface of the water, bleeding badly from several nasty wounds, and really thought that we had lost him. The whole zoo instantly went into mourning. But we patched him up, and the following day Trumpy, minus a few feathers and with a few scars, was his old self again, stalking solemnly round the grounds and greeting everybody.

It was Trumpy who always used to follow the last visitors out, and once he even got on the bus with them to make sure that they were going to go the right way. Trumpy's end was as unexpected as could be, and affected Shep very much because he was responsible for it. He was carrying a large and heavy sack of sawdust on his back as he walked into the mammal house. Unbeknownst to him, Trumpy was trotting, as was his habit, close at heel. Shep, without looking round, dropped the sack of sawdust when he reached the appropriate cage; Trumpy was right underneath it and was killed instantly. We were all very upset by this, but we have since procured two more Trumpies and they are allowed the run of the grounds. They haven't, as yet, developed the personality of the first one, but we hope that they might in time.

Another great character was Dingle, a Cornish Chough. These strange members of the crow family are black with scarlet legs and a long curved scarlet beak. Dingle had been hand-reared as a baby and so was perfectly tame. When he first arrived we kept him in the flat for a few days, but

after he had broken his eighth glass I decided that the time had come when Dingle must be banished to one of the outdoor aviaries. But he was a most endearing bird and liked nothing better than to have his head scratched, whereupon he would crouch on the ground or on your lap, his eyes closed, shivering his wings in ecstasy. He liked to sit on Jacquie's shoulder and run his beak delicately through her hair, presumably in the hopes of finding the odd woodlouse or some similar delicacy, and one day, when he was sitting on my shoulder and I wasn't concentrating on

what he was doing, he rammed a piece of paper into my ear – presumably some frustrated nest-making attempt – and it required a pair of tweezers to get it out again. Dingle bore no malice at being banished to an aviary and still comes down to talk to you and to have his head scratched through the wire.

Of the birds that talk, we have quite a number. We have a parrot, Soocoo, who says, 'Good night, Soocoo,' to himself as the lights are switched off last thing at night. And we have Ali, the Hill Minah, who can say, 'Where's Trigger?' and 'Oooo, he's a good little boy!' But probably the best talker of all is a smaller Minah called Tuppence. If you go up to Tuppence's cage and talk to him he will laugh and giggle, and if you push your finger through the wire and rub his tummy, he will close his eyes and say 'Oooo, that's nice! Oooo, that's nice!'

Lots of people have asked me whether I think that birds that talk really know what they are saying. I'm not quite sure what the answer is. Take Tuppence, for example. He says 'Oooo, that's nice,' when you scratch him because, presumably, that is what his former owners used to say to him when they scratched him, and so he associates the sounds with the actual scratching. But one day he did something which almost made me believe that he knew what he meant. Mr Holly, our ancient and much respected gardener, was trimming a hedge near Tuppence's cage when he suddenly cleared his throat and spat. Immediately, Tuppence, in a clear and penetrating voice said, 'You dirty old man.' Mr Holly was vastly amused by this and went round for the rest of the day chuckling to himself.

There are, of course, numerous stories about parrots, most of which are highly suspect. But there are two I know in which it seemed that the parrot was doing more than just repeating sounds it had learned. The first concerned a parrot that was owned by some friends of mine who lived in Greece. This parrot was taken out every day and put in his cage in the shade of the trees. One day a peasant had tied up his donkey on the other side of the hedge and presently, as donkeys will, it threw up its head and gave its lugubrious bray which went on and on, ending in the great snort that donkeys give when they have performed their solos. The parrot had listened to all this with great care, its head on one side, and as soon as the donkey had finished braying it said, quite clearly and in terms of interrogation, 'What's the matter, darling?'

The other parrot story is of the African Grey Parrot that was the pet of some friends of mine in Athens. He had quite a large vocabulary – in Greek, of course – and his owners were very proud of him. This was in the days when they used to have 'At Homes', that is to say once a week all your friends knew that they could drop in for tea; it was round about the early nineteen hundreds. One day they were having one of their 'At Homes' and the topic of conversation was the parrot and his vocabulary. There was one member of the party who insisted that parrots couldn't talk at all. They merely made unintelligible sounds, he said, and their proud owners immediately exclaimed, 'Listen to what the parrot said. It said so and so.' Holding his tea in one hand and his slice of cake in the other, he walked up to the parrot's perch, looked at the bird, and said, 'You can't talk, Polly, can you?' The parrot regarded him for a moment, and then, in that curious chameleon-like way they have, walked down the perch until it reached him, put its head on one side, and said, in clear and unmistakable tones, 'Kiss my behind.' The effect upon the party was one of stunned shock. The parrot had never used the phrase before and, indeed, never used it again, but it had said it as clear as a bell and there was no getting round it. But the amusing effect was upon the man, who put down his tea and his cake, took his hat and his stick and, white with rage, left the party, saying he wasn't going to stay in a house where guests were insulted.

It is during the winter that the birds usually cause us more concern than all the other animals put together, especially the ones that live in paddocks or aviaries, for these have to be watched carefully to make sure that they don't either suffer from the cold or, what is worse, get frostbite. Bad frostbite on, say a flamingo or something like that, can result in one having to amputate several of its toes. The worst winter that we ever had was that of 1962/3. It was unprecedented in Jersey's history. There was about two feet of snow on the ground, and the ground itself was frozen to a depth of about two feet. As well as all our own birds we had to worry about, we got a constant stream of wild birds being brought in, that were exhausted through lack of food. There were starlings, robins, thrushes, blackbirds, in an unending stream. We did the only thing possible, which was to close the bird house completely to the public – not that there was any public in weather like that – and simply release there all the wild birds that were brought to us. At least it had warmth, and we would place great piles of food on the floor. At one time we had as many as forty coot and twenty-five moorhens, a bittern and two swans, as well as all the smaller fry, all loose at the same time in this small area. It was during this very cold winter that there came, one day, a knock at the front door. When I went to it, there standing on the doorstep was an extraordinary beatnik-like character. He had long sideburns, he obviously hadn't shaved for a considerable length of time, his hair was greasy and matted, he was wearing filthy, shabby clothes, and he looked as though he hadn't washed for all of his nineteen years. He was holding, one under each arm, a pair of coot.

''Ere, mate,' he said to me. 'Can you do anything for

these poor little bleeders?'

To say I was astonished is putting it mildly. I took the birds, examined them and found that they had both been shot, but no more than winged, a mere flesh wound, which would soon heal. However, they were very weak and thin. I looked at the beatnik accusingly.

'Have you been out shooting?' I inquired.

'Naw,' he said. 'It wasn't me. It was some bloody Frenchman. I saw 'im bag these two, and I saw the poor little bleeders weren't dead, so I went and got 'im. Then I took 'is gun away from 'im, and I gave 'im what for. I don't think 'ee'll be 'unting again in an 'urry.'

'Well, we'll certainly do what we can for them,' I said. 'It was kind of you to bring them to us. We've got forty of them already.'

'Oh, that's yer problem, mate,' he said cheerfully. 'Anyway, ta very much.'

And he stumped off through the snow. I thought, as I watched him walk away, how wrong it was to judge people by their appearance. If he'd been in an identity parade he'd have been the last one that I'd have picked out as having a heart of gold beating under that grubby exterior.

Another disaster that nearly overtook us was when the oil tanker, the *Torrey Canyon*, went down, causing such an uproar in the papers and drawing the public's attention to the great dangers of oil pollution, particularly to sea birds. Day by day we anxiously followed the news of the gigantic oil slick. Presently, to our horror, the tide and wind started to turn it towards the Channel Islands. Soon it was heading straight for us. Now I knew that if it did hit us it would not only probably put an end to the gannet and puffin colonies on the Channel Islands, but also that we would have to be prepared to try and cope with hundreds, if not thousands, of oiled sea birds. With all the goodwill in the world we simply had not got space in the zoo to cope with more than about forty or fifty. Something had to be done, and done quickly, so I phoned up Animal Shelter, which is the local equivalent of the RSPCA, and told them what I thought was going to happen. They said they could cope with about forty or fifty birds themselves. Obviously this wasn't going to be enough to deal with the holocaust I visualized, so I phoned up Saranne Calthorpe and asked her if she would come round and see me and form some sort of a plan of campaign. This she did, and in a very short time she had, like a brilliant general, organized the whole of the island.

A large map of the island was put in the office and different coloured pins were stuck in at different points. Some indicated where search parties would go out regularly along the beaches and coves, others indicated the picking-up areas of the birds, and other coloured pins showed areas where we could keep the birds. Everybody rallied round with enormous enthusiasm. The Boy Scouts and the Girl Guides and the Sea Scouts all acted as patrols, as did a number of private people who had the time to do it. Several people with vans or cars acted as bird transport officers, and we found numerous sheds and barns where birds could be kept. In one instance we found a hotel and the managing director very kindly gave us the loan of their swimming pool which, when surrounded with wire netting, could cope with anything up to a couple of hundred birds. Then we waited grimly for the oil slick to reach us. But, by some quirk of fate, the winds and currents changed, and although the tail end of the slick just flicked one or two of the Channel Islands and did a certain amount of damage, the main bulk of it slid past us and headed for the French coast. We had, I think, only about half a dozen oiled birds to treat, so all our preparations had been in vain, but at least we felt that we would

have been ready for the emergency if it had arisen. When
the slick eventually hit the French coast, the French were,
it seemed, completely unprepared and thousands of sea
birds died in consequence.

One fine spring day I was feeling in a particularly benevolent mood, and so I set forth in search of Shep. Whenever you couldn't track Shep down by the intercom system
that we have all over the zoo, you knew perfectly well
where to find him; he'd be in what was called Shep's
field. It is a large water-meadow down by the swannery;
a field sloping due south and shaped somewhat like a bill-
hook with a stream running along the sharp edge. This
stream Shep had dammed up into a series of small ponds
and it was here that he did all the breeding of his birds. In
the ponds he bred his ducks and geese, and on the high
ground his pheasants. Now of all the birds, pheasants
are Shep's chief love, and this particular year he had
done extraordinarily well. I went down to the field in the
spring sunshine. There was the usual cacophony of sound:
the cackling of the geese, the quacking of the ducks, the
thin cheep-cheep-cheeping of the baby pheasants in their
pens, their foster mothers, bantams or chickens according
to the size of the babies, clucking proudly round them. I
found Shep whistling cheerfully to himself, his Alsatian
and his miniature schnauzer close at its heels, peering into
a cage containing a number of little balls of fluff that were
running to and fro and in and out of a bantam's legs as
she clucked to herself and pecked at the ground.

'Morning,' I shouted as soon as I was within hailing
distance, and Shep looked round.

'Morning, Mr D.,' he said. 'Come and look at these.'

I went and peered at the animated balls of fluff as they
scuttled about their foster mother.

'What are they?' I inquired, for most baby pheasants
look very similar at a casual glance, and I usually had

difficulty in telling one species from another.

'They're the Elliot's,' said Shep proudly. 'They hatched out last night. I was just letting them dry out and then I was coming up to tell you.'

'Marvellous!' I enthused, for Elliot's Pheasants are one of the species that are on the danger list, and might well be extinct in the wild state.

'Eight hatched successfully out of eight eggs,' said Shep. 'I never expected that proportion.'

'They look all right to me.'

'Well, there's one that looks a little bit wobbly, but I think he'll be all right,' said Shep.

'I came down to give you a piece of news,' I began. 'I've decided that as you've done so well this year, I'll buy you any pair of pheasants that you like, that come on the market, and are of interest to you. I don't mean the zoo or the Trust will buy them. I will buy them personally, as a mark of my esteem for your noble efforts.'

'Gosh, really?' said Shep. 'Thanks very much, Mr. D.'

Little did I know, when I made this rash statement, what I was letting myself in for.

Every morning, when the mail is sorted, there are the inevitable lists from dealers in different parts of the world, telling us what creatures they have got for sale. These are piled on my desk and I skim through them, keeping a careful eye out for anything that is particularly rare and of value to the Trust. On this particular morning I skimmed through the lists but didn't happen to notice what was on one of them. All the lists were returned to the main office, where the staff, in turn, would look at them. Presently there came a knock on my door and when I shouted, 'Come in,' Shep's face poked round the corner.

'Can I see you a moment, Mr D.?' he said. He looked white and strained, not at all his normal cheerful self.

'Come in,' I said. 'What's the problem?'

He came in, carrying a dealer's list in one hand, and closed the door.

'Did you see this list?' he asked in hushed tones.

'Which one is it?'

'Jabira.'

'Yes, I saw it,' I said. 'Well . . . why? What's on it?'

'Didn't you notice?' he said. 'White-eared pheasants.'

'Are you sure?'

'Quite sure,' said Shep. 'Look . . . Here.'

He put it on my desk and pointed. There, sure enough: 'Expected shortly, White-eared pheasants'. No price was given. This was an ominous sign as it usually meant that the animal in question was expensive. In the case of the White-eared pheasants I knew very well that they would be. Firstly, they are one of the largest and most spectacular of the eared pheasants. Secondly, they are probably extinct in the wild state. And, thirdly, as far as one knew, there were only seven birds in captivity anywhere in the world, and most of those were in America. I sighed. I knew perfectly well that they were birds that the Trust should have, and I also remembered my promise of the previous day to Shep.

'Well,' I said, resignedly, 'you'd better phone them up straight away, because the other zoos will be on to them like weasels on to a rabbit. But, you understand they've got to be a reasonable price, Shep. I can't go paying the earth for them.'

'Oh, no,' he said. 'I realize that.'

He got on the telephone and presently was through to Holland.

'Mr van den Brink?' he said, and his voice cracked with emotion. 'I phoned up about the White-eared pheasants on your list.'

There was a long silence while he listened to what van den Brink had to say.

'I see,' he said. 'I see.'

He turned imploring eyes on me and put his hand over the mouthpiece of the telephone.

'He hasn't got them yet, but they're on the way. And he wants two hundred and fifty pounds each for them.'

I groaned inwardly, but a promise is a promise.

'All right,' I said. 'Tell him we'll have a pair.'

'Mr van den Brink,' said Shep, his voice shaking, 'we'll have a pair. Will you reserve a pair for us, please? Yes, that's right, Jersey Zoological Park . . . And you'll let us know? You'll give us some warning before they come, won't you? . . . I see; they'll be coming via Paris . . . That suits us very well. Thank you very much indeed. Goodbye.'

He replaced the receiver and started pacing up and down the office, looking extremely harassed.

'Well, what on earth's the matter with you now?' I said. 'I told you you can have a pair of them. What are you looking so glum about?'

'Well . . . Well, I think it's unsafe just to have one pair,' Shep blurted out.

'Now, look, dear boy,' I said. 'That's five hundred quid I've just spent on a pair of pheasants for you. I really can't afford to buy another pair.'

'No, no! I didn't mean *you*,' said Shep. 'I meant *me*. Would you let me buy another pair? It would be far safer if we had two cocks and two hens.'

'But Shep,' I protested, 'it's five hundred quid! Have you got that amount of money?'

'Oh, yes,' said Shep, impatiently, 'I've . . . I've got the money. It's . . . it's, will you let me buy them?'

'Of course I'll let you buy them, if you want to spend your money on them,' I said. 'But it's a lot of money.'

'It's a lot of risk if we only have one pair, and lose the cock or the hen,' said Shep. 'So I can do it?'

'Of course you can, but you'd better phone up right away.'
So within minutes he was back on the telephone.

'Mr van den Brink? About those White-eared pheasants of yours . . . We've decided we'll have two pairs instead of one . . . Yes, two pairs . . . Thank you very much indeed. Goodbye.'

Shep put back the telephone and looked at me with exultation on his face.

'Now, with two pairs, we should be able to do something,' he said.

But the buying of the birds was only the start, for now two aviaries had to be built for them on clean ground — that is to say ground upon which no other bird had been kept so that there could be no risk of infection being left in the soil. This was done, and we waited impatiently for the arrival of the White-eareds. Weeks and weeks passed, and periodically we would phone Mr van den Brink who was very apologetic but said that as the birds had to come from Peking, through Moscow to East Germany and then, from there, to Paris and thence to us, it was quite a complicated procedure. He would get them to us as fast as he could. Then the great day dawned when he phoned us and said that the birds had arrived in East Berlin and would be dispatched the following day. Shep was remarkably agitated that day and couldn't concentrate on any conversation that anybody had with him. He was waiting, with the utmost desperation, to see what condition the White-eareds were in when they arrived. At last, they came from the airport. We stripped the sacking from the front of the cage and saw our two pairs of White-eared pheasants: beautiful, big, white birds, with long fountain-like tails of white feathers, scarlet cheeks and black top-knots. They were incredibly handsome and we gloated over them. Then we carried the cage carefully down to the two aviaries that had been prepared for them, and released a pair in each aviary.

Three of the birds were extraordinarily wild and Shep said he got the impression they must be wild-caught birds and not ones that had been bred in captivity. The fourth bird, however, was remarkably docile. This was one of the cock birds. He was so docile, in fact, that we began to get a little suspicious. But Shep fed them and gave them water and, as they were so nervous, we covered the aviary with hessian so that they wouldn't be frightened by any members of the public passing close by. The following morning Shep and I went to look at them, and the docile cock bird was even more docile; in fact, so docile that it was obvious that there was something wrong with him. But while we were phoning up Tommy Begg to get his advice, the bird died. Tommy came and did an immediate post-mortem examination, and we soon discovered the cause of death. The bird's lungs were riddled with aspigilosis. This is a particularly virulent form of fungus disease which, once it attacks the lungs, spreads with ferocious rapidity, and for which there is no known cure. The bird might have lived, even in that condition, for some years, but the long and arduous trip had been too much for it. It had stirred up the lung complaint and the bird had died in consequence.

'I think it was a good idea of yours to get two pairs,' I said, gloomily, to Shep.

'Yes,' he said. 'You know, I had a feeling that something like this might happen. Wouldn't it have been awful if that had been one of the only pair that had been sent?'

I couldn't have agreed with him more.

Now we were left with two hens and one cock bird, but as far as we could see they were all in very good condition and so we had high hopes that we might be able to breed from them. They had the whole of the summer and the following winter to settle down, and by the spring they had become comparatively tame. The cock bird seemed to fancy one hen bird more than the other, and so we ran those two regularly in one aviary and kept the old hen separately. Then, one morning, Shep came bursting into my office, carrying in his arms the female White-eared pheasant.

'Good God,' I said. 'What's the matter? She hasn't gone and scalped herself or anything, has she?'

For pheasants have a habit, when they are frightened, of flying upwards like rockets and hitting their heads on the wire tops of the cages, sometimes scalping themselves completely.

'No, it's worse than that,' said Shep. 'She's egg-bound.'

The bird had obviously been straining for some considerable time to pass the egg, and was in a very exhausted state. We gave her some glucose and water, and I phoned up Tommy Begg. He told me to give her a shot of penicillin and then try all the normal remedies for easing the egg out intact. So we injected her, and then, with the aid of oil, steam from a boiling kettle, and every remedy we could think of, endeavoured to extract the egg. But it was no use. It was impossible to do, and the bird was far too exhausted to help us. There was only one thing to be done, and that was to break the egg inside her and then remove it piecemeal, a very dangerous procedure which might well lead to peritonitis, as we all knew. We succeeded in getting the egg out, and all the contents, and gave her a gentle enema with warm water just in case there had been any bits that had escaped our notice inside. Then we put her in a dark box in a warm place and left her, we hoped, to recover. But a couple of hours later she was dead. Shep and I stood looking down at her body.

'Well,' I said, attempting to look on the cheerful side, 'we've still got a pair, at any rate.'

'Yes,' said Shep. 'We've got a pair, I suppose. But he doesn't really fancy that hen, you know.'

'Well, he'll just jolly well have to fancy her,' I said.

So we put them in together. It was too late for them to breed that season, so we waited for the following spring anxiously. By this time they had settled down quite well together and the cock bird seemed to be showing certain signs of affection towards the hen. Then, one morning, Shep came into the office, looking as gloomy as he could possibly look.

'It's the White-eareds again,' he said.

'Oh, God, not again!' I said. 'Now what's happened?'

'You come and look,' he said.

We walked up to the aviaries and stared in. There was the cock bird limping around so heavily that I thought, for a moment, he must have broken his leg. It was Shep's guess that during the night something had frightened him and he had flown up, and as he fell backwards had caught his toe in the wire and wrenched the muscles in his thigh, possibly damaging some of the nerves. Shep and I looked at each other and we both knew what we were thinking. A cock pheasant, unless he has the use of both legs, finds it very difficult, if not impossible, to tread the hen successfully. Unless we could cure the leg it looked as though we had no chance of breeding the White-eared pheasants. With great reluctance we caught the cock bird and I examined his leg and thigh. It was not dislocated at the hip, nor were any of the bones broken, so our original diagnosis that it must be a sprain gave us some hope that it might clear up. We gave him an injection of D.3, a product that we found effected miraculous cures in the paralysis that you sometimes get in monkeys' hind limbs, and watched his progress day by day. But he didn't seem to get any better; he just hobbled around the cage, barely putting his foot on the ground, and then only the tips of his toes just to keep his balance. I never said anything to Shep, and Shep never said anything to me, but both of us, in our heart of hearts, were convinced that our efforts to breed the White-eared pheasants were doomed to failure.

5. Leopards in the Lavatory

Samuel John Aliru
c/o Phillip Ansumana
R.C. School
Bambawullo

Dear Sir,

I am here asking you kindly to develop my 221 Kodax film which I am here sending with my brother Phillip Ansumana. If you are able to undertake the developing and printing please do so.

I would have come with him but I am just composing a song and which I hope to present it to you next week.

I am also a scholar and I attend the Wesley Secondary School at Sezbwema.

                Yours truly,
                Samuel John Aliru
Respondez s'il vous plait.

For some considerable time I had been endeavouring to persuade the BBC to film an animal-collection trip, but they had been very myopic about the whole thing. I tried to convince them that the fascination of the trip lay not only in catching the animals but in keeping them as well, and then bringing them back by sea. I felt this would all make excellent film material. However, they dithered about it for a year or so, before eventually saying yes. I was delighted, as I thought it would be excellent for the Trust. First of all, the publicity would be considerable; secondly, the Trust would be obtaining some nice animals for its collection; and, thirdly, though hitherto I had had to find the money for all my expeditions myself, the BBC would at least be assisting me with financing this one. The Trust at that time, although doing very well, could not afford to start indulging in collecting trips.

We first thought of going to Guyana, but the political unrest there at the time made it seem a rather unwise spot to choose. I had once been caught in a revolution and had been forced to let half my animals go; and I didn't want this to happen in the middle of filming a series for the BBC. After some thought I decided on Sierra Leone. It was a part of West Africa that I had never visited, it contained some particularly rare creatures which the Trust could do with, and also I happened to love West Africa and its inhabitants very much indeed. I was delighted when the BBC said that Chris Parsons was going to be the producer. He was an old friend of mine and I had worked with him before; in fact, we had done a mammoth trip through Malaya, Australia and New Zealand together, and I knew and liked him enormously. So I went over to Bristol and we formulated our plans. I decided that I and a member of the staff would go out by sea, arrange the base camp, and catch as many animals as we could in the shortest possible space of time, and then the camera crew and Chris Parsons would fly out to join us. We worked it out so that we would have about a fortnight for collecting before they arrived. It was essential to have some animals already caught for some of the film sequences when they arrived. Then I had to decide which member of the staff to take with me. I picked John Hartley, otherwise known as Long John. He is six foot two high and immensely thin, so that he looks rather like a Cruikshank caricature, but he was young and a hard worker and he was wildly enthusiastic when I suggested it to him.

Then came the very necessary but rather tedious process

of collecting all the equipment that we would need for the trip. You are never quite sure, on a trip like this, what will be obtainable in the country itself, and so as to be on the safe side you have to make yourself almost entirely self-supporting. We took hammers and nails, screws, traps and nets and cages of various sorts, babies' feeding-bottles in case we got any young animals, hypodermic syringes and various medicines in case any of the animals got ill, and a host of proprietary products such as Complan, a sort of powdered milk which we found was very useful for rearing baby animals. When this had all been accumulated it made quite a considerable pile. Then, as always seems to happen when you are organizing an expedition of any sort to anywhere in the world, a snag arose. We discovered that no ships that called at Freetown would carry animals. In desperation I phoned Elder Dempster and spoke to one of the directors. Luckily he had read some of my books and had liked them, and so they kindly waived their rule about carrying animals on passenger vessels. They said that we could not only go out on the *Accra* but come back on her too and bring all our animals with us.

So, on a bleak, grey, drizzly day at Liverpool docks, Long John and I got our mountain of luggage on board the *Accra* and we set sail that evening. Jacquie had decided not to come with me. She had been to West Africa twice and the climate didn't agree with her at all. Instead, she was going off on her own with Hope Platt and Ann Peters, my secretary, for another visit to the Argentine.

It was rather good that during the course of our voyage we ran into one of the worst storms possible. Storms at sea do not worry me in the slightest and I am never seasick, but I was interested to see whether Long John would be. It is no fun having to look after a lot of animals if you are going to be seasick. Luckily, Long John proved to have a stomach like iron and we didn't miss a single meal. We spent a lot of our time in the smoking-room, relaxing, drinking beer, and looking at all the books we had brought with us on West African fauna and memorizing the habits of the creatures that we hoped to collect. Long John would lie spread out in his chair like a ship-wrecked giraffe but, as I pointed out to him, the voyage was the only time that we would have for relaxation so he'd better make the most of it while he could. I also told him that he would have to be prepared to rough it. I drew gloomy pictures of grass huts full of spiders and scorpions, hot beer, having to bathe out of a bucket, and similar terrors of the tropics.

We arrived at Freetown on a beautiful, blistering hot day, and the lovely aromas of West Africa were wafted across the sea to us; smells of palm oil, flower scents, and rotting vegetation, all combining into a lovely, heady mixture.

I had been lucky enough to obtain an introduction to Mr Oppenheimer through a Mr Geddes, who is a Trust member, and he had instructed the Diamond Corporation of Sierra Leone to give me all the assistance I required. I knew that we would have to spend some time in Freetown and so one of the things I had done was to write ahead and ask whether they could either book us rooms in a hotel or, if it was possible, get us a small flat somewhere. I was somewhat embarrassed when a chauffeur, in immaculate livery, came on board as soon as the ship had docked and asked me if I was Mr Durrell. I said yes, and he said he had got the car waiting to drive me to one of the Dicor flats, as they call them, which had been put at our disposal during our stay in Freetown. I hadn't expected much because I had been warned that accommodation in Freetown was cramped and pretty hot and sticky. I asked him to wait while we got all our luggage through Customs, which was done with the utmost efficiency. In fact

I think it is the only Customs shed that I have ever been in and out of in so short a space of time with such a mountain of varied goods. We piled these into the back of the enormous four-wheel drive truck that Land-Rovers had kindly lent to us, and I got into the posh-looking car with the chauffeur while Long John drove the truck behind. We drove through the town and then, a little way outside it, came to a pleasant area where the houses were set well back in gardens that were a riot of flowers. Presently we went up a curving drive, aflame with hibiscus bushes, and there was a great glittering block of flats. I looked at them in astonishment.

'Is this the place?' I asked the driver.

'Yessir,' he said.

We drew up in front of the flats and immediately stewards in white uniforms appeared and took our bags up to the third floor where we were ushered into a flat that took my breath away. To begin with, it was enormous; the main living-room could have held about fifty people. Secondly, it looked like a Hollywood set. Thirdly, it was air-conditioned, and fourthly, from the veranda that ran along the front of the living-room, you had a magnificent view right down over the hills to Lumley Beach, one of the best beaches in Sierra Leone, that stretches for miles.

'Well,' said Long John, looking around, 'this is a bit of all right, isn't it? I don't mind this sort of grass shack, if this is what you meant.'

'I didn't mean anything of the sort,' I said severely. 'You wait till we get up country; then you'll really have to rough it. This is just a little bit of . . . er . . . extra, as it were. We're very lucky to have it.'

I wandered into the kitchen and found the steward in there. He stood smartly to attention.

'Are you the steward?' I inquired.

'Yessir,' he said, beaming. 'I am the steward for this flat.

My name is John. I am also the cook, sir.'

I glanced round the kitchen, which was gleaming and immaculate, and spotted in one corner an enormous fridge.

'I suppose,' I said tentatively, 'I suppose you haven't got any beer, have you, John?'

'Yessir! Yessir! I bring it straight away, sir.'

I went back to the living-room and sat down in a chair, still a bit bewildered by all this luxury. Long John came sauntering in. He'd been exploring the rest of the flat.

'There're three bedrooms,' he said, 'and all of them are almost as large as this room. It's incredible.'

'Well I've discovered that there's some iced beer,' I said. 'So I don't suppose we'll starve.'

We had a great number of things to do and people to see. I had to get the permits for collecting animals, and for their export, and make contact with various people we thought might be helpful to us when we were up country. The awful part about this was that our enormous Land-Rover was classified as a lorry, and the same applied even to the smaller one. Lorries are not allowed in the interior streets of Freetown. This problem, however, was solved by the kindness of the District Commissioner, who put a car and a chauffeur at our disposal.

Then we had to decide where we were going to make our base camp and, after some deliberation, I decided that the focal point should be the town of Kenema, some four hundred miles up country. I chose it because it was quite a sizeable town and therefore would make the getting of food and supplies more easy, and also because the Diamond Corporation had an office there and, as they were being so helpful to us, I felt that if they were within reach it would be a good thing. On the *Accra* we had met up with Ron Fennel, who was working in Sierra Leone as adviser to the government and had suggested Kenema to me originally. When I had asked him whereabouts he thought we might be able to form a reasonable base camp, he said, 'Why don't you try the chrome mines?' At first I thought he was joking. I didn't really fancy living in a mine. But he went on to tell me that some five or six miles from Kenema itself there were some chrome mines and a lot of empty houses which had been built for the miners and their families. The chrome had given out and the whole place was now deserted. He felt sure that I could get official government sanction to take over one, if not two, of these houses and live in it. I thought this an excellent idea and eventually tracked down the official in question who promptly gave me the permission I required.

I don't like cities as a rule but Freetown I found enchanting. The streets all had the most delightfully incongruous names, such as St James's, The Strand or Oxford Street – all terribly British. English colonists are wonderful. Give an Englishman a swamp two thousand miles from anywhere and he will, in a blaze of originality, call it Piccadilly. Charming London buses ploughed through the streets carrying vast quantities of Africans, and on every side there were great skyscrapers, like white honeycombs, standing next to the remnants of the old Freetown, beautiful, large weatherboard houses. By and large I preferred the old architecture to the new, but they seemed to blend in well together.

The next thing we had to do was to try and organize some staff, and so I made my first contact with Sadu. His name had been given to me by a friend who had spent several years in Sierra Leone and had employed him. He said that Sadu was an excellent cook and, moreover, was honest and a hard worker. Sadu himself turned out to be a tiny wizened little man, with a face rather like a monkey's and an impish grin. When he had settled on his salary, I told him to go to the town and search for a 'small boy'. Now a small boy, in West African parlance, means a sort of second-in-command. He's really the boy who peels the potatoes, makes the beds, and does all the dirty jobs, while your cook – or the steward, if you've got one – does the less menial tasks. Presently Sadu returned with Lamin, who was a boy of about fourteen, very shy, with a charming grin. We employed him on the spot. Then came the great day. All the documents had been stamped and signed and sealed, everything was ready, and the large Land-Rover (the small one was being left in Freetown for the BBC team) was piled up with all our gear, with Sadu and Lamin installed in the back. We climbed into the cab and drove off up country.

The first part of the drive was magnificent. Smooth mac-adam roads, and all the trees and bushes hung with flowers, red, yellow, purple and white, and then – at mile ninety-three – BANG! we hit the laterite. Red dust was plastered all over the plants and the trees on the roadside, and this fine red dust gets into your eyes and lungs and everywhere. It has the consistency of talcum powder and can slither through the tiniest crack. The corrugation in the laterite, caused by the winter rains and the wind, make the vehicle shudder so that after a few miles you feel as though you've been riding on a pneumatic drill for at least three hundred years.

The road seemed to wind on for ever, and the dust to become thicker and thicker. Occasionally, we would pass through a palm-leaf thatched village and all the young children would run out, eyes shining, teeth glistening, to wave pink palms to us in greeting as we passed. Sometimes a pair of hornbills would fly across the road, their wings flapping madly, their long beaks making them look top heavy. One got the impression that they had to flap their wings so wildly since otherwise the weight of their beaks would make them nose-dive instantly to the ground.

After some hours of driving, we reached the village of

Bambawo. The chrome mines lay in the hills behind Bambawo, but it was in the village itself that we were supposed to pick up the caretaker who had the keys to the various houses. This we duly did. Then we branched left and wound up into a low range of hills which lay behind the village. As we climbed higher the road got worse and worse, but the forest became more magnificent because this was real forest, not secondary undergrowth; gigantic trees standing on huge buttress roots covered with orchids and various epiphytes, and great waterfalls of giant ferns. As the forest grew thicker, my thoughts on what type of accommodation we were liable to find up there got more and more gloomy. Then we rounded a corner and there were the chrome mines. They were completely and utterly unexpected. First there was quite a large administration block. We drove past this and saw that there was a swimming-pool – empty, of course, and full of dead leaves, but a pool nevertheless. The road wound up a little higher and then, spread out along the top of the hillside, were some seven or eight beautiful little villas, each one tucked away amongst the trees, and each commanding the most magnificent view down over the plain in which the village of Bambawo lay, and across hundreds of miles of thick forest to the Liberian border. A lot of the houses had, of course, been allowed to go to wrack and ruin but we discovered two, both commanding magnificent views, quite close together and in excellent condition.

While our things were being unpacked and stacked in the house, I discovered from the caretaker that the administrative block contained a dynamo to produce electricity for this little village, and that, if we cared to obtain the necessary oil and petrol to work this, what he referred to as the electro-shitty man would be only too happy, for a small sum of money, to come up and run the dynamo for us. So this was organized, and I also arranged for two stalwarts from the village to clean out the swimming-pool and fill it. Long John and I spent the rest of the day unpacking our things and putting them in heaps in various parts of our spacious accommodation, and then, that evening, we sat down to an excellent curry which Sadu had produced.

'You know, this was the part I was dreading most,' said Long John, sipping his cold beer appreciatively. 'The grass shack stuff, you know, scorpions in the roof and the spiders, warm beer . . .'

'You just shut up and concentrate on your food,' I said. 'We've been damned lucky. I've never had a camp as luxurious as this. Do you realize that we have a bath and a lavatory that really work? That's the height of luxury.'

We soon found that the chrome mines had other treats in store for us. For example, the water that we got came from springs in the forest just a little way behind the houses and so was pure enough to drink without our going through the awful tedious process of having to boil and filter it first. Also, there were no mosquitoes; we were high enough to catch every cool breeze that was going and so it never became oppressively hot in our houses.

The next few days were fairly hectic. We had an interview with the chief of Bambawo, a kind elderly man, to explain to him why we had come and to ask him if he could enlist the aid of the villagers for catching us 'beef'. 'Beef' is the term which is used in West African pidgin to describe any animal from frog to an elephant. We then engaged a carpenter and set him about the task of building a series of boxes to which we could attach the cage fronts which we had brought out ready-made from England. Very soon we had an impressive row of cages, all completely empty. We then drove to every village within a twenty mile radius and spread the tidings of our arrival and of what we were trying to do; saying that we would return in three days' time to see if they had managed to capture any beef for us.

We had returned one evening from what Long John called one of our whistle-stop tours, had bathed and changed and eaten in self-satisfied silence, and were just relaxing preparatory to going to bed, when we heard a curious noise coming from down the hill; the sound of pipes and drums and chanting. Presently we saw a line of people coming up the road below us with their hurricane lights flickering as they passed through the trees.

'Who on earth can they be?' asked Long John, for the road led nowhere but to our house.

'I don't know,' I said. 'I suppose it's some sort of deputation from the village. Perhaps the chief's sent his band up for us, or something.'

We waited patiently, and presently the crowd of singing, chanting Africans appeared round the side of the house and lined up in front of us on the veranda. Two men in their midst were carrying a pole across their shoulders and from it was dangling quite a substantial cage made out of rough logs.

'Ah!' I said to Long John. 'This looks like our first beef. Now, whatever it is, don't get too excited over it, otherwise the price will go up.'

'No, I won't,' promised Long John. 'I'll try and pretend that it's something so revolting that we wouldn't have it even if they gave it to us.'

'Now, what you get, my friends?' I asked the assembled crowd.

'Beef, sir. Beef!' came an immediate chorus from the crowd, and their teeth shone white in the lamplight as they grinned proudly at us.

They had put the cage at our feet and we tried to peer through the logs to see what was in it. It was big enough, I thought, to contain quite a large animal. However, we could see nothing, so we moved it into the light and cut through the bush ropes that had been used to tie down the lid.

'Careful, sir!' said one of the hunters, as I gingerly lifted the edge of the lid to see what the cage contained. 'This beef go bite you.'

I lifted the lid a bit more and peered into the large box. Then, suddenly, in the crack appeared the most appealing face. It was a tiny Spot-nosed monkey who would have fitted conveniently into a large teacup, and his little green face had a heart-shaped white spot of fur on the nose. His eyes glistened and he peered at me through the crack. Then he uttered the piercing squeak of the baby monkey that was to become such a familiar sound in camp. I threw back the lid and lifted him out. He had a greenish body, a long tail, and a wistful face. He clung to my fingers tenaciously and uttered another tremendous wail.

'Dis beef no go bite,' I said to the hunter. 'Dis no be big monkey, dis be picken monkey.'

I knew this ploy of old. For some obscure reason the Africans always imagine that if they could make out the animal they brought you to be more savage than it was, you would automatically pay more for it. I handed the baby monkey over to Long John, who enveloped it gently in his enormous hands and held it while I got on with the bargaining. This was a protracted business and I eventually beat the man down from five pounds to two pounds. This was really far in excess of what the baby monkey was worth, but I have always found it a good policy to start paying a little more than you should for the first animals in order to encourage the hunters to go and get more; then you can drop your prices. So, eventually, well pleased with their bargain, the group left us, singing and chanting and beating on their little drum. They disappeared down the hillside, while Long John and I went and got some warm milk and fed the baby monkey, who was terribly hungry. Then we gave him a nice warm bed of dried banana leaves in one of our cages and left him for the night.

'Well,' I said to Long John, as we climbed into bed, 'that's our first beef. Not such a bad one at that. Spot-noses are quite rare. Maybe it augurs well for the future.'

During the next week the news of the price we had paid for the monkey spread, as I had anticipated, and soon there was a steady trickle of hunters coming up to the house with a strange assortment of beasts. There were bats and baby owls, brush-tailed porcupines, more baby monkeys, giant rats the size of a kitten, and mongooses in a variety of shapes and sizes. Also, our whistle-stop tours of the villages round about had paid dividends and when we went to visit them again we rarely came away empty handed, even if it was only a tortoise or a young python that they'd managed to catch for us. Our cages were full of whistlings, rustlings, squeakings and hootings, and we felt that by the time the BBC arrived we would have a nice collection of animals with which to greet them. However we had not as yet got our two prime objectives for coming to Sierra Leone: one, the beautiful Colobus monkeys, the other, leopards. Then, just before the BBC arrived, we did get our leopards, but in the most unexpected way.

I had questioned all the hunters carefully as to the possibility of getting some of these beautiful cats which are becoming increasingly rare throughout their range, owing to the fact that they are shot for their skins. All the hunters shook their heads and said that leopards were 'hard too much' to catch. I began to think that we weren't going to get any, when one day a very battered Land-Rover appeared winding its way up the road towards us. When it stopped, a lanky young American with curly hair got out and introduced himself as Joe Sharp. He said he worked with the Peace Corps in Kenema, and he had heard we were animal collecting. Would we, by any chance, be interested in a pair of leopards?

'I'd say we would! Why? Do you know where there are some?'

'Well,' he answered, laconically, 'I've got a pair myself. I got them off a hunter and hand-reared them. They're about six months old . . . I thought you might be interested in them.'

'I certainly am,' I said eagerly. 'Where are they?'

'They're here,' he said, gesturing towards the back of his Land-Rover.

He walked round to the back of it and opened the door, and out jumped two of the most beautiful leopards I've ever seen. They were each about the size of a large labrador retriever, beautifully marked, with sturdy legs, and their skins shone in the sunlight as they wound themselves round Joe Sharp's legs, purring loudly. They were each wearing a collar and to these Joe attached two leads. We led them round to the front of the house, tied them up on the veranda and sat gloating over them.

'They're called Gerda and Lokai,' said Joe, stretching himself out in a chair and accepting the beer that I offered him. 'I think they must be brother and sister because they were brought in by the same hunter at the same time, and they were both approximately the same size, although you'll see Gerda's a little more slender than Lokai.'

Lokai had put his paws on the table and was sniffing at my beer suspiciously. He then peered earnestly into my face and gave my hand a quick lick with his rasplike tongue.

'Well, they're yours if you want them,' said Joe. 'I don't want to part with them, really – I've got very fond of them – but I'm going back to America shortly and it would be impossible to take them back there.'

'We certainly will have them,' I said. 'I think they are the most handsomely marked leopards I've ever seen. Are they completely trustworthy at the moment?'

I said this because, at that precise juncture, Lokai had got down from the table and wrapped his paws affectionately round my leg. I could feel his claws digging into my skin.

'Well,' said Joe, 'now there's a point. They're OK with me, and they're OK with some of the other guys down in the Peace Corps. But there are one or two they've taken a dislike to, and then they get a bit funny. Lokai likes to jump on you from the top of a door, for example, and if he hits you at the wrong angle he's quite a weight.'

'If he hits you at the wrong angle I should think he could break your neck,' I said, disentangling Lokai's paws from my leg with difficulty.

'Oh, I think they'll settle down all right,' said Joe. 'They're very nice-tempered, really.'

'Where,' inquired Long John, putting his finger on the crux of the whole problem, 'where are we going to keep them?'

The thought hadn't occurred to me. It was the carpenter's day off, and in any case we hadn't got a crate big enough to take them. One would have to be specially built, which meant a trip into Kenema to get sufficient planks to do it. All this would take time, and the BBC were arriving the following day. I thought about the problem for a moment, and then I remembered that just between our house and the little house farther down the hill that the camera crew were going to occupy, there was a small hut, measuring some six foot by ten and about nine foot high, which I presume at one time had been used as a sort of staff lavatory. If that was cleared out, I thought, the leopards would be quite happy in there until we could get

a proper cage made for them. We went down immediately to inspect the hut and found that it was perfectly adequate for the leopards, except that there was a gap between the roof and the top of the wall of about eight inches. But Joe assured me that they wouldn't be able to get out of that.

So we took Gerda and Lokai down to their new quarters, after they had been cleaned out, and gave them a large plateful each of their favourite tinned dog food which Joe had been rearing them on. Then we left them to their own devices and went back to have another beer. That evening, after Joe had left us, Long John and I, in some trepidation, carried down the leopards' evening meal. As soon as they heard us approaching they set up such a series of yowls and purrs and scratchings at the door that Long

John and I looked at each other in alarm.

'I think,' I said, 'I think we ought to be armed for this operation.'

So we cut ourselves two stout sticks just in case.

'Now,' I said, 'I think if we open the door cautiously and push one bowl of food in, that will keep their attention occupied and we can get the other bowl in and the dirty bowls out.'

'Yes . . .' said Long John, doubtfully.

We opened the door slowly and cautiously, and immediately the leopards flung themselves at it, snarling with satisfaction at the smell of the food. We pushed the plate in hastily, and it skidded across the floor into the far corner, the two leopards chasing madly after it. Then we whipped in, got the dirty plates out, put the second plate of food on the floor, and made a hasty retreat, slamming and bolting the door behind us.

'Whew!' said Long John. 'They're going to be a bit of a handful, aren't they? The sooner we can get them into a cage the better.'

'We'll have to get cracking first thing tomorrow,' I said. 'If you go into Kenema and get the planks, I'll persuade the carpenter to do some overtime. He should have the cage ready by tomorrow evening, I should think. It's quite a simple construction, anyway.'

'Righto,' said Long John. 'But I don't fancy feeding them in the morning. I might not be alive to get to Kenema.'

'Well, there's nobody else who can do it, so we'll just jolly well have to.'

'Ah, well,' said Long John. 'I suppose it is what would be classified as a hero's death.'

And on this sombre thought we went to bed.

The following morning, by the same rather complicated process, we fed the leopards and then, when they had finished, cautiously opened the door and peered at them. They were lying there licking their lips and purring with gentle satisfaction. It seemed as though the food had had a soothing effect upon them. As we had to get on intimate terms with them in any case, I thought this was as good a time as any. So Long John and I locked ourselves in the lavatory with the two leopards and talked to them and stroked them. Gerda seemed to show an immediate preference for Long John, and Lokai for me. That is, if you can call putting his two fat paws on my knee and then stretching himself and yawning and digging all his claws into my kneecap, a sign of affection. After half an hour of this we put some fairly lengthy ropes through their collars and took them out for a little walk. They behaved very sedately and really looked magnificent in the sun. When the time came to take them back, however, we had a bit of a struggle, but fortunately, with the aid of another plate of food, it ended without any bloodshed.

Long John set off to get the wood in Kenema, and some other supplies we needed, while I finished cleaning and feeding the animals and awaited the arrival of the BBC team. They arrived simultaneously with Long John, for they had met up in Kenema. Long John had obviously filled them full of stories of what a ghastly place we were living in, for when their Land-Rover drew up and Chris got out of it he was wearing an expression of disbelief on his face.

'Lucky devil! I see you've fallen on your feet again,' he said, grinning, as he came towards me.

'Well, it's not bad. It's a modest little place,' I said, 'but it's got all mod. con. and that sort of thing. And after all, there's plenty of jungle at the back there that we can film in.'

'Lucky devil!' he repeated.

Chris is a man of about medium height, with a very

prominent nose, the end of which looks as though, at some time or other, it had been chopped off. He has heavy-lidded, green eyes, which he tends to hood like a hawk when he is thinking, and in moments of crisis he retreats behind his nose like a camel. He introduced me to the other two members of the team. There was Howard, who was short and stocky with dark curly hair, and enormous horn-rimmed spectacles which made him look like a benevolent owl – and Ewart, the cameraman, who was tall, blond and rather Scandinavian looking. We all sat down and I asked Sadu to bring us some beer.

'How did you find this place?' asked Chris.

'Pure chance,' I said. 'The whole place is deserted; it's like a sort of village Marie Celeste. But we've got all the necessities of life. Bathrooms in both the houses – which *work*, and the lavatories work, too, which is even more important. And we've got a fridge so we can have cold drinks and keep food. And we've also got electricity, which would be rather useful, I thought, for charging the batteries for the cameras and so forth. Also, just down the end of the road there, there's a swimming-pool, if you boys are feeling energetic.'

'Good God,' said Chris. 'It's incredible!'

'It is. It's the most fabulous base camp I've ever had in all my days of collecting. I've never had such luxury.'

'Well,' said Chris, raising his glass. 'Let's drink to the chrome mines.'

'They're not called the chrome mines any more,' said Long John. 'They're called the beef mines.'

And from then onwards that is exactly what we called them.

When we'd finished our drinks I took them down to show them their living quarters. As we passed the lavatory I waved at it in an airy fashion.

'By the way,' I said, 'don't go and unbolt that door,

will you? There're a couple of leopards in there.'

'Leopards?' said Howard, his eyes growing wide behind his spectacles. 'You mean . . . you mean . . . leopards?'

'Yes. You know, those spotted things,' I said. 'We've got them locked in there until we've got a suitable cage ready for them.'

'You sure they can't get out?' said Howard, in trepidation.

'No, no. I don't think so for a moment,' I said. 'Anyway, they're quite young and tame.'

After lunch, Ewart, Howard and Chris went down to their house to unpack and check the recording and photographic gear, to make sure that no damage had been done to it over the rough roads. Long John was busy giving milk feeds to all the baby animals, and I was writing a letter. Suddenly, there were shouts of, 'Gerry! Gerry!' and a distraught-looking Howard came panting up the hillside, his spectacles all misted over with emotion.

'Gerry!' he called. 'Come quick! Come quick! The leopards have got out!'

'Dear God!' I said, and leapt to my feet.

Long John dropped what he was doing instantly, and arming ourselves with sticks, we went down the hill after Howard's palpitating figure.

'Where are they?' I inquired.

'Well, they were sitting on the roof of the lavatory when I left. Chris and Ewart were standing guard.'

'God save us,' I said. 'If they get into this forest, we'll never catch them again.'

When we got down there we found Chris and Ewart, armed with sticks and looking extremely apprehensive, standing at a discreet distance from the lavatory, on the top of which was perched Gerda, snarling in a gentle sort of way to herself. But there was no sign of Lokai.

'Where's Lokai gone?' I asked.

'He jumped down a minute ago. I couldn't stop him,' said Chris apologetically. 'He's gone off in that direction.'

He pointed down the hill towards the swimming-pool.

'John,' I said, 'you handle Gerda. She likes you better than me. But for God's sake don't do anything silly. See if you can get her down . . . or get up to her and get a rope through her collar. Chris, you come with me and we'll look for Lokai.'

Chris and I went down the hill and searched and searched, but I really thought that Lokai had turned off into the thick forest that lay behind us, and that we would never see him again. Then, suddenly, we spotted him lying placidly under a small orange tree. Slowly I approached him, crooning sweet nothings, and he purred at me in a friendly sort of way. With somewhat tremulous hands I slipped the rope through his collar and tied it securely. Then I handed the end of the rope to Chris.

'Here. You wait here with him,' I said. 'I must go back and see how Long John's getting on with Gerda.'

'What do I do if he moves?' called Chris plaintively to me as I ran back up the hill.

'Follow him,' I shouted back. 'But don't try to stop him.'

When I got back to the lavatory, Ewart and Howard were still dithering in the background with their sticks, while Long John had found a box and had climbed up and managed to get the rope through Gerda's collar. So at least we knew she was secure from that point of view. But for some reason she seemed in a bad mood, and disinclined to come down from the roof of the lavatory. In the end we had to get a long pole and push her gently towards the edge, until she had to leap to the ground, where she turned and snarled at Long John as though he were responsible and made a vague patting motion with her paw. Now, although these leopard cubs were only six months old, it must be remembered that they were lethal animals, and a playful swipe from one of their paws could easily take away half your face. So it was with great circumspection that we urged Gerda to go back into the lavatory. Once we'd got her back inside, Long John sat with her and talked to her and stroked her, and she seemed to calm down considerably. I then went back down the hillside to find Chris, looking like a forlorn stork, holding on to the rope from the other end of which Lokai was regarding him with a somewhat baleful stare. I took the rope away from Chris and gently pulled Lokai to his feet.

'Come on, Lokai,' I said. 'Come on . . . Nice food . . . Gerda's waiting for you. Come on . . . lovely lavatory. Come on . . .'

And by this means, slowly, with many pauses to smell at things and look around and admire the view, we managed to get Lokai back to the lavatory.

In the meantime, the carpenter had been alerted and had brought planks which he nailed round the gap in the roof so that there could be no repetition of this escape. We all went back up to the house and had a beer to soothe our shattered nerves.

'I hope that sort of thing doesn't happen every day,' said Ewart.

'Well, not every day,' I said. 'On an average, about three or four times a week, you know. But then, after all, that's what you're out here to film, isn't it?'

'You can't keep them in there indefinitely,' said Chris. 'What are you going to do with them?'

'The carpenter's in the process of building a cage for them now. It should be ready by tonight, and then we've got to get them into it. That's going to be another jolly little lark.'

'Good lord! What a wonderful film sequence that'll make,' said Chris.

'Well, he won't have finished the cage till after dark.'

'That's all right,' said Ewart. 'We can rig up the lights

'As long as the lights don't frighten them,' I said. 'If they start getting too nervous, I'm afraid you'll have to stop the whole operation and switch them off. I'm not risking my neck for the BBC.'

'Yes, all right,' said Chris. 'I promise that.'

So the rest of the afternoon was spent bringing up lights while the carpenter put the finishing touches to the handsome cage he'd made for the two leopards. By the time he'd finished it was quite dark, and we switched on the lights experimentally. They were very powerful indeed and lit up the whole area with a great glare that I felt was not going to be the most soothing thing that a leopard had ever seen. Eventually, when everything was ready, Long John and I, armed with platefuls of dog food and our ropes and sticks, went down to fetch the leopards up the hill. First we pushed the food in and then, when they'd finished it, we went in and talked to them soothingly, told them they were going to be film stars, put the ropes through their collars, and led them out. Gradually we moved up the hill, letting them make the pace. They loved to stop and stare, and their ears would twitch and you could see their whiskers come out almost as though they were antennae. Slowly we moved on and came over the brow of the hill and into the glare of the searchlight.

One moment Long John was with me, the next he wasn't. He was off, tearing down the hillside, with Gerda dragging him along as though he had been a puppet. There was nothing I could do because I was attached firmly to Lokai, and he didn't seem to have the same feelings about the searchlight as Gerda did. I led him slowly up and towards the cage. He'd never seen a cage before, so he was naturally a little suspicious. I allowed him to walk round and sniff it, and then I put a plate of dog food inside and urged him in. I got him half-way through the door when he suddenly decided that this was a dastardly trick I was playing on him and tried to back out. But luckily he had an ample behind and with a quick push I managed to get him in and slam the door. Then, when he was eating, I got the rope detached from his collar and out of the cage. By this time a panting Long John had appeared on the horizon dragging a reluctant Gerda with him. She was in a filthy temper and we now had the problem of trying to get one leopard in a bad temper into a cage containing another leopard who showed every desire, having finished his food, of wanting to come out again. It took us some time to accomplish this, but at last we managed it, safely slammed the door on both of them and heaved heart-felt sighs of relief. From behind the searchlight came Chris's voice.

'That was a marvellous sequence,' he said enthusiastically. 'And it went off so smoothly. I don't know what you were all so worried about.'

Long John and I, drenched in sweat, covered with scratches that had been playfully delivered by the leopards *en route*, stared at each other.

'What I say is,' said Long John, with conviction, 'blast the BBC.'

'Motion carried,' I said.

6. Catch Me a Colobus

Dear Sir,

My wife was born in the hospital. Doctor has written me to go and pay for her. If you will pay us today I will go. If you are not going to pay us, please sir trust me the sum of (Le.4) or £2. I dont want to go without your notice.

Good morning sir.

By now the collection had increased considerably, and in addition to everything else we had three boisterous young chimps that we had got from people round about who had been keeping them as pets. One was called Jimmy, one Amos Tuttlepenny and the third Shamus NoTool. The size of the collection meant a lot of extra work, and Long John and I had to get out of bed at dawn so that we could have all the animals clean, fed and ready for filming by nine o'clock or nine-thirty when the sun was up and the light was right.

Curiously enough, getting out of bed at dawn in the beef mines was a pleasure rather than a penance. Our view stretched south over three to four hundred miles to the Liberian border, and the whole of this in the early morning looked as though it had been drowned in a sea of milk with just the odd hills sticking up here and there like islands. The sun would come up in a spectacular fashion like a frosted blood-orange, and then, as it gathered heat, it would draw up the mist into long coiling skeins so that it suddenly seemed as though the forest, as far as you could see, was on fire. After we'd had a cup of tea and admired the dawn, we'd do the routine check along the line of cages, to make sure that none of the animals had sickened for something awful during the night, and then Long John would get on with feeding the baby animals on milk or whatever it happened to be, while I would start cleaning the cages. When this was done we would spend an hour or so chopping up fruit and various other things for the animals. Then it would be breakfast time and the camera crew would come, yawning and stretching up the hill, and join us. Once breakfast was over we would discuss what the film sequence of the day was going to be, and set about it.

All filming is, of course, a fake, but there is faking and faking. In our case, if we wanted to show how an animal was captured, we would take it out of its cage back into the forest and then 'recapture' it for the sake of the film. Or if we wanted to show how an animal behaved, we would again take it out into the forest, put it in an appropriate setting with nets around, and then wait until it behaved naturally in the way we wanted it to. This was sometimes tedious work and took a lot of patience, specially when you had to stand in the red hot sun.

On one occasion, I remember, we wanted to film a pouched rat feeding and then, when he couldn't eat any more, stuffing his cheek pouches full of food for future reference. This gave them the appearance of suffering from an acute attack of mumps. Pouched rats are not the most attractive of animals; they are about the size of a half-grown cat, with large pinkish ears, a mass of quivering whiskers and a long, pinky-brown tail, and their fur is slate grey. We had one called Albert who always gorged as much as he could as soon as his food plate was put in the cage, and then would stuff his cheek pouches full of whatever was left and take it over into the corner where his bed was and bury it. I felt sure that if Albert was taken out into the forest he would repeat this process for us, so when the morning came Albert was kept without his breakfast and then solemnly transported down to the buttress roots of a giant tree. We rigged up the nets, arranged a nice selection of forest fruits on the floor and released Albert.

To our consternation, the cameras were grinding away

and Albert was ambling in amongst the fruit, yet he didn't seem in the slightest bit interested in it. He found a nice little niche in the buttress roots of the tree, curled up and went to sleep. We hauled him out ignominiously and put him back amongst the fruit, and he repeated the whole performance again. Four times we did it; four times Albert took no notice of the fruit whatsoever, although by this time it was long past his breakfast time and he must have been hungry. Then, on the fifth occasion, he suddenly (almost with a start) noticed the fruit. He sniffed at one of them eagerly and then, instead of doing what I'd promised Chris he would do, picked it up daintily in his mouth, retreated to a corner, and squatting on his hind legs, ate it with all the delicacy of a dowager duchess eating an ice cream. It was not at all what we wanted, but at least it provided some material.

On another occasion we wanted to film a potto. These are strange little Teddy-bear-like creatures that are distantly related to the monkeys. They have the most extraordinary hands, the forefinger of which has been reduced to a mere stump to give them an extra grip on the branches of a tree, and they also have the vertebrae on the neck sticking up in a row of little spikes through the skin. The potto's method of defence, when attacked, is to duck his head between his forelegs. When whatever is attacking him tries to grab him by the neck, it gets a mouthful of these sharp little spines, which acts as a deterrent to any but the most determined predator. We wanted the potto for what is called a 'matching shot', to fit in with another sequence that we had filmed the day before. All he had to do was sit on a branch, and then walk along to the end of it. We didn't demand very much of him. He'd had his supper, so he wasn't hungry, and we thought that by placing him on a convenient branch we would get the whole scene finished in about five minutes. We found the right sort of branch in the right sort of position, rigged up the lights and the cameras, which took quite some time, and then the potto was brought up and placed on the branch. He immediately ducked his head between his forelegs and went into his defensive position, and there he remained. A quarter of an hour passed, and the lights were getting too hot so that we had to switch them out. Still the potto remained immobile. I could not imagine why he should suddenly be afraid of us, because he would readily accept food from one's hand, but for some reason or other he seemed terrified of the whole procedure. So we left the lights switched off and squatted there, waiting patiently.

Now a tropical forest at night is for me one of the most

beautiful things I know, and this forest was a particularly beautiful spot. In the rainy season the ravine was obviously a foaming torrent of water, but now it was dry and the great boulders were covered with wigs of moss, and all over these flew and crawled hundreds and hundreds of brilliant emerald-green fireflies. Little ghostly drifts of moths would pass by you, and all round were the cries of the various cicadas and other insects, ranging from noises like a buzz-saw to somebody ringing a very, very tiny bell. Absorbed by all this I almost completely forgot the potto and the BBC, until Chris whispered in my ear.

'I think he's going to move.'

We got to our action stations, the lights were switched on, the potto raised his head slightly, and then ducked it again between his forelegs. Another quarter of an hour went past and then, suddenly, two things happened simultaneously. Firstly, the potto started to look up, and at that moment Ewart looked at his watch and made what I think must have been the most incongruous remark made in Africa since Stanley met Livingstone.

'They'll just be coming out of the pubs in Bristol now,' he said thoughtfully.

This had an instantaneous effect upon the potto, who, I feel, must have been a Temperance leader for, instead of running along the branch towards the camera, he turned tail and fled in the opposite direction. It took us about half an hour to catch him in the maze of branches. At last we recaptured him and put him back on the branch, and then he behaved beautifully, and we got the bit of film we wanted. But it had taken well over two hours to get a sequence which on the screen only lasted for possibly thirty seconds.

Of course, we also filmed the daily routine of cleaning and feeding the animals, though nobody could possibly describe looking after a collection of animals as routine

work. They do their best to irritate and amaze you every day. For instance, we had a very handsome African kingfisher. Well, we couldn't supply him with his natural food (which consisted of small lizards and snakes and a certain number of grss-hoppers and locusts) in sufficient quantities, so we had to teach him to eat meat. But whenever he took a strip of meat he insisted on killing it by banging it on his log vigorously before he would eat it.

As I had ... ed Long John, there comes a time on every collecting tr ... This is a ... en you begin to think that you know it all. ... it all, howeve ... t of great danger, for you *never* know pompous and ... you try. It is when you start getting are liable to m ... about your own abilities that you thinking I knew ... stake. I made a mistake once by wasn't a pleasant ... d got bitten by a snake, which cautious. But one d ... e. It taught me always to be a most enchanting b ... came in, bringing with him ... was a young White-crested hornbill. Now these birds are predominantly shiny coal black, but the feathers on their heads are fluffy and pure white so they look as though they are wearing a sort of cottonwood hat. I was delighted with this because it was the only hornbill that we had got so far, and I gave Long John a long lecture on hornbills and their ways. Baby hornbills and baby toucans are usually easy to rear, and I felt convinced that with Tommy, as we called him, it would be a walk-over. Shortly after his arrival, we chopped up some nice fruit, put Tommy on the animal table and dangled bits of fruit in front of his nose. He took not the slightest notice of it.

'He'll get used to it in time,' I said, 'but I suppose to begin with we'd better force feed him.'

We pushed a lump of fruit down Tommy's throat, which he promptly regurgitated. We pushed another lump farther down, and after some minutes he managed to regurgitate that, too.

'Perhaps he hasn't settled down properly,' I said to Long John. 'We'll leave him in his cage for a bit and then return. After all, we don't know when the hunter got him. His mother may just have fed him and he isn't hungry.'

So we put him back in his cage. Two or three hour later we got him out again and went through the same laborious process, but every time he regurgitated the fruit. We continued trying to feed him on fruit throughout the day, and he wouldn't have it at all.

'I can't understand it,' I said to Long John. really can't Most baby hornbills go mad after the first of feeds and you can't give them enough.'

By the following morning Tommy was beginning to look anything but bright and, although he seriously hungry, he still refused his fruit. g for it. I'll go

'Damn it,' I said. 'There's only be something and look him up in the book.'

funny about what they feed on.'

Now I, in my ignorance, was under the impression that all hornbills fed upon things like vegetables, fruit and insects, so they could be called, as it were, omnivorous. But when I looked Tommy up in the book I found that he was one of those very rare hornbills that fed almost exclusively off meat. What we'd been trying to do was stuff a lot of fruit down him which he didn't like at all – rather like thrusting a raw steak down the throat of a convinced vegetarian. So we got Tommy out of his cage, put him on the table, chopped up a nice selection of meat, and within about thirty seconds he was gulping it down wolfishly. From that moment onwards he never looked back. It taught me a lesson, and I hope it taught Long John one, too.

It's one thing to look after an animal in a well conducted zoo where you have everything at your command, both from the feeding and the veterinary point of view, but it's a different kettle of fish when you are sitting five hundred miles from nowhere, with all your animals in little wooden boxes, and you have got to be everything from veterinary surgeon to maintenance man; and of course the animals, as soon as they have accepted captivity, start exhibiting all their eccentricities for your edification. It's curious the fads and fancies your animals develop. One day they'll go mad for oranges, for example, so you immediately increase your supply and shower oranges upon them. The next day, if you give them an orange, they look at you as though you had mortally offended them and decide that they would much prefer peanuts. But unless you indulge them, as you would indulge an elderly lady with her pekinese, they will not be happy and they will not thrive.

We had, at one stage, a Scaly Anteater, or Pangolin,

brought in to us, which pleased me greatly because in the past, when I had collected in West Africa, I'd never had any success with these curious beasts that look like animated fir cones with tails. This was because they feed principally upon the ants that build their nests in the trees, the ferocious little black tree ants. I had given the question of the pangolins' diet some thought while I was in England and had decided that, although they would take raw egg and milk and mincemeat as a mixture, something was obviously still lacking, and that something must be a trace of formic acid. So on this occasion I had brought a small bottle of formic acid out with me in order to try it, and I made up the mixture for the pangolin every day. I often wondered, as I was doing it, how a TV cook would describe the recipe:

'Take two tablespoonfuls of powdered milk, darlings; beat it up into a quarter of a pint of water, and when this is of a smooth creamy consistency, add one raw egg and beat briskly until it is thoroughly mixed. Then place into this a handful of finely minced raw meat; stir gently, and finally garnish with a small portion of chopped tree ants' nest and a drop of formic acid. Serve immediately. You will be delighted with the effect that this recipe will have on your guests, and will, without doubt, be the most popular pangolin party thrower of the season.'

It would, I reflected, be interesting to do a sort of cookery book for the animal collectors; a kind of *Larousse Gastronomique* dealing with the best way of serving maggots and so on.

By this time we had filmed most of the animals in the collection, and the rolls of film were mounting up, but we still hadn't found two of the animals that we had specially come to Sierra Leone to get, the Red-and-black and the Black-and-white Colobus monkeys. The hunters would bring us in monkeys of every other description, and in the end I began to despair.

'It's no good,' I said to Chris. 'We'll have to organize a couple of monkey drives and see if we can't get them that way.'

'What are monkey drives?' inquired Chris, puzzled.

'Well, they do them down on the cocoa plantations,' I explained. 'They drive all the monkeys into a certain area, and then they kill them because they raid the cocoa

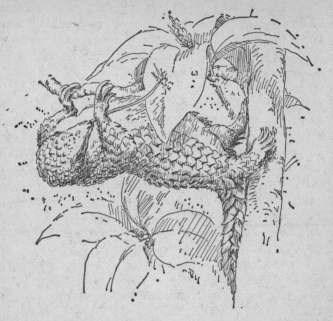

crops and ruin them. They're paid a bounty of a shilling a head, I think, by the government. I'll send Long John into Kenema this morning and get him to find out the best areas which they think we can operate in. It should make quite an interesting film sequence, actually.'

So I sent Long John into Kenema and he returned, in due course, telling us he'd got the names of three or four villages where monkey drives were held fairly regularly, but that we would have to go and see the Paramount chief of the area to get his assistance before we could persuade the villagers to organize a monkey drive out of season. We decided to go and see the chief the following day, and organize the monkey drive as rapidly as possible.

Next morning I got up at dawn as usual and wandered out on to the veranda waiting for Sadu to bring the tea.

Long John never appeared before the tea; he clung to his bed like a limpet. I was standing, looking out over the misty forest, when I heard some noises in the valley just below the house. I knew it was monkeys because there was that lovely sound as they leap into the leaves, like the crash of surf on a rocky shore. But I couldn't see, at first, exactly what kind of monkeys they were. They were heading for a big and rather beautiful tree that grew a couple of hundred yards from the veranda just below us. It had a sort of greeny-grey trunk, the leaves were a very vivid green, and it was covered, at this time of year, with bright cerise-pink seed pods about six inches long. There was another crash and rustle amongst the leaves. Then silence for a moment. And then, suddenly, it seemed as though the whole tree had burst into bloom, a bloom of monkeys. They were Red-and-black Colobus, and they were the most breathtaking sight. They had rich, shining, chestnut-red and coal-black fur, and in the morning sun they gleamed as though they had been burnished; they were magnificent. There must have been a dozen or so with a couple of babies, and it amused me the way the babies would use their parents' tails or the branches of the tree quite indiscriminately, as a means of hoicking themselves from one place to another. To my surprise, they were not feeding on the seed pods but were stuffing themselves with vast quantities of young leaves and shoots of the tree. They were, without doubt, some of the most beautiful monkeys I'd ever seen, and I was determined that we were going to add a few to our collection, come what might. They stayed in the tree, feeding quietly and uttering little cries to each other, until Sadu suddenly arrived on the veranda with a great rattling tray of teacups. When I looked back at the tree they had all disappeared. As I sat sipping my tea, I remembered a stupid woman I'd met at a cocktail party in Freetown, who'd said,

'I cannot understand why you're going up country, Mr Durrell. There's absolutely nothing to do or see there.' I wish she could have seen those Colobus.

Later that day the team and I set off to interview the Paramount chief and elders of an area quite close to our village, leaving Long John behind to look after the animals. The Paramount chief and elders were having a meeting of some sort and we had to wait until this was over before we could have an audience. The chief himself was quite a young man and very handsome, dressed in plain white robes and a multi-coloured skull-cap, whereas most of the other elders were wearing flamboyant robes of different colours. I described, through an interpreter, why we'd come to Sierra Leone and, in particular, that we wanted to film, and catch alive, the two species of Colobus monkey. But I had to keep stressing the 'catch alive' part, because they were so used to killing the monkeys that they couldn't quite grasp the fact that we wanted them alive and unhurt. I finally convinced the elders and the chief of what we wanted, and I hoped that they would tell the various villages and put the message across in no uncertain terms. Both the chief and the elders were delighted. They had such mobile, such beautiful faces. Their great black eyes were as cold and calculating as any street vendor in Petticoat Lane, but they could break into life at the slightest joke, when they'd glow and flash with an animation that is, by and large, totally lacking in a European. The chief said to us that, if we wanted merely to film the various types of monkeys, he thought one of the best places was a cocoa plantation not far from the village. There, he said, there were plenty of monkeys of all different kinds. But it wasn't a good place to hold a monkey drive. We'd have to go to a village some way away for that. Since we were there, however, we thought we'd take a look at this cocoa plantation.

As we drove along to it, I gave some thought to the monkey situation in Sierra Leone. Every year, between two and three thousand monkeys are killed in monkey drives. This is due to the fact that the monkeys, unfortunately, have not been told about the importance of the cocoa crop to Sierra Leone's economy, and so they pour into the cocoa plantations and do a great deal of real damage; therefore, of course, they have to be controlled. It is unfortunate, however, that every monkey suffers from this. When they organize a monkey drive in Sierra Leone, the participants are paid a bounty for the head of each monkey and every species is indiscriminately killed. This includes the two species of Colobus that we were after, in spite of the fact that these were, theoretically, protected by law. Here you had the situation, and a typical one, where one man was being hanged for another man's crimes, because the Colobus, in fact, does no damage to the cocoa plantations at all. It was the same situation that I had seen all over the world and which always sickens me; governments ready to pay out millions of pounds for airy fairy schemes, but not a penny towards animal conservation. So you get the situation where three thousand monkeys are slaughtered per annum, half of which have committed no crime against the cocoa crop and which could, in fact, be a valuable tourist asset.

As soon as we arrived at the cocoa plantation I could see why monkey drives were necessary. On all sides there were large troops of them feeding in the young cocoa trees. But, as I had suspected, they were mainly Spot-nosed and Diana monkeys; not a single Colobus amongst them. When you saw the nurseries of young cocoa trees all laid out in regimented rows, you could quite see that a cocoa tree two or three years old could be completely stripped by a rowdy troop of monkeys in about ten minutes.

Chris and the others had set up the cameras and were

filming the Spot-nosed and Diana monkeys in the trees, so I walked to the outskirts of the plantation and soon found myself in the forest. There's no real demarcation line but eventually when you can no longer see any cocoa trees, only indigenous forest and the giant rustling bamboos spout up like solidified fountains, you realize that you are outside the plantation. Walking through these bamboos was a strange experience, for in the slightest breeze their great trunks – which are as thick as a man's thigh – would creak and groan musically. It must have sounded like that rounding the Horn in an old sailing ship in a high wind. I was looking for Colobus monkeys, but the trouble is that in the tropics you are inclined to forget your objective because every step of the way is so filled with interest. You see a flower that you've never seen before, or a brilliantly coloured fungus or moth, or an equally brilliantly coloured tree frog or grasshopper. The tropics have been designed like a flamboyant Hollywood epic to make you realize how tiny and insignificant you really are, and how complex and beautiful the world is that you live in.

I walked quietly through the forest, pausing now and then to examine something that caught my eye and, suddenly, to my delight, I achieved my objective. There was a rustling crash ahead of me in the trees and, moving quietly towards it, I found myself just below a group of Black-and-white Colobus. It was quite a small group, consisting of about six individuals, and one of the females was carrying twins, which was very unusual. They were feeding quietly among the branches some fifty feet above me, and although they knew I was there they showed no fear at all. Looking at them through my field glasses I discovered that they were not nearly as colourful as the Red-and-black Colobus, but with their jet-black fur and snow-white tails, and a picture-frame of white fur round their faces, they had all the quiet dignity of some strange religious order.

Eventually, when they had fed enough in that tree, they moved off. Now, I'd thought that the Red-and-black Colobus were pretty agile in the trees, but the Black-and-white ones had them beaten hands down. Without apparently even thinking, they would hurl themselves from the top of a one-hundred-and-fifty foot tree and crash into the branches below with a grace and precision that would make Billy Smart burst into tears of joy. I walked back to the plantation, where I found Chris quite exuberant for once since they'd got some excellent shots of Diana monkeys and Spot-nosed monkeys feeding. Then we packed up our gear and made our way back to the village.

It was market day, and I love African markets so much that we stopped and wandered about a bit. Everyone was so busy and so predatory, their beautiful eyes glowing, their teeth shining, everyone in their Sunday best – the most vivid colouring. Piles of multi-coloured fruit and vegetables, long rows of highly-coloured bundles of cloth : it was just like walking through a rainbow. There was nothing, it seemed, that you could not buy, from dried frogs neatly skewered on slivers of bamboo, to sandals made out of old motor car tyres. As we were wandering about I was suddenly approached by a slim young man wearing a battered solar topee, white singlet and khaki shorts. He raised his topee politely and said, 'Are you Mr Dullell, sir?' in such a shrill squeaky voice that for a moment – in spite of his garb – I thought he was a woman.

I admitted that that was who I was.

'The chief has sent me, sir,' he said. 'I am Mohammed and the chief has told me that you want to catch monkeys alive. Now I, sir, can organize it for you.'

'Thank you very much,' I said, cautiously, because he didn't look to me the sort of man who could organize a monkey drive. Nevertheless, if the chief had sent him to me, he must know what he was doing.

'When would you like to do a monkey drive, Mr Dullell?' he went on.

'As soon as possible. The monkeys I want to catch particularly are the Colobus – the Black-and-white and the Red-and-black. You know them?'

'Yes, sir, I know them,' he said. 'There are plenty here, plenty.'

'How, actually, do you do these monkey drives?' I inquired.

'Well, sir,' he said. 'First we find the monkeys, very early in the morning, and then we drive them, we drive them, we shout, we drive them, and we shout more, and then we drive them, until we get them to the right spot. Then we cut down all the trees all round. Then we must build, at the bottom of the tree in which the monkeys are, a coop.'

'A coop? What on earth's a coop?'

'We pile all the branches on the ground at the foot of the tree – a great big pile, you understand – and then the monkeys come down the tree and they go into the coop, and you catch them.'

It sounded highly unlikely to me, but I could tell, from the seriousness of his face, that he meant what he was saying.

'When could we organize a drive?' I asked.

'The day after tomorrow I can do it.'

'Fine,' I said. 'And we want to be there when you actually start, so that we can film everything. You understand? So you mustn't start without us.'

'No, sir.'

'We'll be there about nine o'clock.'

'Oooohhh . . . that's very late, sir,' he said.

'You see, we can't film before then because there's no

light,' I explained.

'Well . . . if we get the monkeys near the proper tree, can you film from then?' he asked me anxiously.

'Yes . . . if there's enough light,' I said. 'If it's about nine o'clock or nine-thirty. Then there'll be enough light for us to film.'

He thought about this for a bit.

'All right, sir,' he said. 'You come to the village at nine o'clock, and I'll have the monkeys ready there for you.'

'All right. Thank you very much.'

'Don't mention it, sir,' he said, and put on his solar topee and strutted off through the crowded market place.

So, two days later, we rose very early. All the camera equipment and the sound recording equipment was carefully checked and we set off for the village where the monkey drive was to take place. When we arrived we were led along a narrow path through a banana plantation, and then some distance into the forest. Gradually, an enormous uproar made itself heard from somewhere ahead of us, and eventually we came to the place where they had got the monkeys. My first impression was that there was a hell of a lot of noise and confusion, and about three hundred Africans hacking down the undergrowth in all directions, with Mohammed strutting about among them shrieking, at the top of his voice, instructions which apparently nobody obeyed. They had succeeded in getting two troops of Colobus into one enormous tree, and they were busy cutting down all the undergrowth that could possibly form escape routes for them. As they gradually sealed off the escape routes, the monkeys began to panic. One or two of them leapt out of the huge tree, hurtling perhaps one hundred and fifty feet down into the top of a palm tree, and escaping; whereupon all the Africans would yell in unison and redouble their efforts.

I hate felling trees at the best of times, and I hated to

see some of these trees go crashing down, but I knew that this area was going to be cleared for a cocoa plantation anyway, so the trees would have had to come down in the end. Finally, the last big tree that could have formed an escape route crashed into the undergrowth, and then all that was left were several palm trees from which they had to cut away the great fronds. As each frond was severed and fell to the ground it made the most wonderful whispering, rustling sound, like somebody curtseying in a stiffly starched crinoline.

By now the efforts of my noble band of hunters had felled a considerable area of forest round the main tree, and I waited expectantly for the next move – which consisted of the African equivalent of a tea break. Some of them cut lengths of a certain creeper which is hollow and contains quite a large quantity of water inside – it's a sort of living well – and these they held up to their mouths and sucked the water from them. They were hot and thirsty and dripping with sweat and they all argued, as they drank from the creepers, about the best way to go about the following stage of the operation. The next thing, Mohammed informed me in his piping voice, was to build the coop. So there was further hacking and sawing and great branches and palm fronds were piled in a conical mass round the base of the tree. This we surrounded with nets. Having done this, the Africans all went into the surrounding undergrowth and cut themselves long forked sticks. These were necessary because, when the monkeys finally came down into the coop and then out of the coop into the nets, one had to have a forked stick to pin the net down over them so that one could get a grip on their head and their tail.

I had been keeping a careful watch on the top of the tree in which the monkeys were congregated, but the foliage was so thick that I couldn't tell exactly how many were up there, although I knew I had the two species of Colobus we wanted. Mohammed told me that everything was now in readiness and, in a spirit of bonhomie rather than conviction, I ordered the cages to be carried up to the front line. I wasn't at all sure that their methods were going to be proved right, but there was just a chance that we might catch the Colobus and I wanted to be prepared. Then two men produced, from God knows where, an enormous and very ancient saw which had practically no teeth at all, and they climbed over the nets, up the coop to the trunk of the great tree, and started to saw at it.

'What,' I inquired of Mohammed, 'are they trying to do?'

'If the monkey thinks that we are cutting down the tree, sir, he go come down to the coop, and then we catch him,' he explained, wiping the perspiration from his brow.

I trained my field glasses on the top of the tree. The sawing didn't appear to be having any effect upon the monkeys. The tree was of an enormous girth and it was quite obvious that it would take the men approximately six months to get through it with that antiquated saw. After half an hour or so I was convinced that their efforts were going to be in vain. I called Mohammed over.

'Yessir,' he said, coming at a run and saluting smartly.

'Look, Mohammed, I don't think we are going to do it this way,' I said. 'The monkeys don't seem to be a bit disturbed by the sawing, and it's going to take them ages to get through that tree. Why don't we try something else?'

'Yessir. What else, sir?' he asked.

'If you clear a small area at the base of the tree,' I said, 'so that the actual coop itself doesn't catch fire, and you light a small fire there and put plenty, plenty, plenty of green leaves on it, then the smoke will go up into the tree and maybe this will make the monkeys come down.'

'All right, sir,' he said. 'We'll try.'

He went off, screaming at the top of his voice like a seagull, and presently a small area had been cleared at the base of the tree and the fire had been lit. I watched the smoke from it coil lazily up, sneaking its way round the trunk of the giant tree, climbing higher and higher. And then I looked to see what the effect on the monkeys was going to be. As they smelt the first few wisps of smoke, the Colobus I could see moved about a bit anxiously, but otherwise did not seem unduly perturbed. But presently, when more green leaves had been piled on the fire, and the smoke grew thicker and thicker and thicker, they began running to and fro among the branches.

Now, in strange contrast to the extraordinary cacophony that had been going on when the undergrowth had been cleared, the circle of some three hundred Africans had fallen absolutely silent and were standing in a ring round the net, their forked sticks at the ready. I was just about to tell Mohammed to impress upon the Africans not all to rush at the first monkey that came down – if, indeed, it did come down – thus leaving practically the whole net unguarded, when a Black-and-white Colobus leapt from the top of the tree, landed gracefully on the coop and, to my astonishment, disappeared inside it. There was a sort of 'Aaahhh' from the Africans, rather like a football crowd when a goal has been scored. There was a long pause and then, quite suddenly, the Colobus popped up and ran straight into the net. As I had predicted, most of the Africans rushed forward eagerly with their forked sticks.

'Tell them to get back into line . . . to get back into line!' I shouted to Mohammed.

He, screeching orders, drove the men back into line, leaving only two of them to deal with the Colobus. They pinned it down successfully under the net, and I ran forward to look at it. By this time one man had got a good grip on the back of its neck and a firm hold on the base of its tail, and was lifting it out of the net. It was a female, half-grown, I judged, and in beautiful condition. Although they look so sombre and so tractable, these monkeys can, in fact, give you a wicked bite, and they have to be handled with great care. We carried her over to one of the cages, put her in and shut the door on her, and then covered the cage with palm leaves so that she would feel more secure in the dark. Then, as I turned back from doing this, the tree suddenly seemed to rain monkeys. They crashed down on to the coop, one after the other, so fast that I couldn't count them, and by the time they were on the coop and I tried to count them there, they'd disappeared inside the branches.

Now there was complete pandemonium. Monkeys were appearing and diving into the net one after the other, and the Africans were pinning them down with their forked sticks and shouting and screaming. The confusion was indescribable. I could do nothing, except stand by the cages and rapidly try to sex and count the monkeys as the Africans brought them to me.

It is amazing, looking back on it, how many things your mind has to think of at once. As each pair of Africans came towards me, carrying a struggling monkey, I would wonder whether they were handling it too roughly or holding it too tightly. Then I'd got to check what sort of condition it was in. If it was an adult, and the teeth were well worn, it meant it was a fairly old specimen; in which case, how well would it settle down in captivity? I had to watch carefully while they put them into the cages because they were tending to slam the doors and catch the monkeys' tails in them. Then I'd be wondering, in the back of my mind, how much shock the animal had suffered? Was it cool enough? Would it survive the journey back to the beef mines? And if I got it back there, how

would it settle down? It was curious that, in spite of tne fact that the capture must have frightened the monkeys considerably, they were most of them accepting food from my hand within a couple of hours of capture.

When the final monkey had been caged, we examined the coop carefully to make sure that there were no more lurking inside the branches. At last I could go and examine my captives individually, and count them. All I knew, up to that point, was that we had been incredibly lucky to catch both the Red-and-black and the Black-and-white in one fell swoop. When I examined the cages I found that we had caught, in fact, ten Red-and-black Colobus and seven Black-and-white, of varying ages and sizes and sexes, which was the important thing. Each cage, carefully covered with palm leaves, had to be lashed to a pole and we set off in a troop through the forest, the men carrying the swaying cages between them in a long line, chanting a gay and triumphant song.

I felt very exultant. After all the weeks of waiting, and all the sweat and labour we'd put into the trip, we'd achieved our final objective, we'd caught our Colobus. But this was only the first stage of the game, I reflected, as the cages were packed into the back of our giant Land-Rover, and we drove slowly over the bumpy road back to the beef mines. Now came the crucial test: could we keep them?

7. Keep Me a Colobus

Sirs,

We will be grateful if you can attend our dance tonight which will be at 9.00 p.m. prompt. The dance is for our sister Regina who joined the police force and is now out. It is just a sendoff dance. You are all invited to this dance.

Awaiting for an immediate reply.

The address is

                J. B. Musa   *Bambawo*

   M.C.   *J. P. Musa*

As I had suspected, catching the Colobus was one thing, keeping them alive was quite another. The chief difficulty was not that they did not settle down to captivity; they were almost resigned to that immediately. The difficulty lay in feeding them. In the wild state they live in the uppermost branches of the trees and feed almost exclusively on leaves, moss and other coarse green matter and, I rather suspect, the occasional bird's egg or lizard forms part of their diet. In consequence, the stomach, instead of being a simple sac as in other monkeys, has developed into a succession of dual lobes to extract the greatest possible nourishment from this rather un-nutritive bulk of food. In many ways these resemble the stomachs of the hooved animals that chew the cud. Often, in the Colobus, the stomach is so large that a quarter of the animal's weight can be attributed to it and whatever it contains.

To begin with we could feed them with the natural foods that we obtained from the forest around us, and they ate ravenously. But this, I suspect, was something to do with the shock of capture because, within twenty-four hours, their appetites had trailed away to almost nothing. We began to get worried indeed. In desperation, we went down to the market in Bambawo, at the bottom of the hill, and bought large quantities of the green-stuffs that the Africans grow to make their stews and food with. There were several different varieties of this – some resembled spinach, some a rather large-leafed clover – and we tried these on the Colobus. To begin with they displayed no interest at all, then they started feeding, in a rather desultory fashion. And then, as though they had decided to accept their fate, all the Black-and-white ones started feeding quite normally on the green-stuff that we got from the market, but the Red-and-black ones continued to eat just sufficient to keep themselves alive. They were so totally different in character that you wouldn't have thought that they were both Colobus. The Black-and-whites were alert and lively and soon tamed down so that they would take food from your hand. The Red-and-blacks, on the contrary, were sullen and morose and seemed to withdraw into themselves in what could only be described as a fit of sulks.

The two things that worried me most were, firstly, that we were shortly due to go back to Freetown to catch the boat home, and secondly, that we had, in some way, to teach the Colobus to eat something other than their natural food – something which we could supply them with on the voyage, like apples, carrots, and so on. Unfortunately, most of these foods were unobtainable in Bambawo or in Kenema. We did manage to obtain some apples at colossal cost, but the Colobus merely sniffed at them and threw them away. In the hope that we might be successful in catching Colobus, I had got the *Accra* to bring out with it large quantities of carrots, cabbage, and every other sort of vegetable I could think of that might tempt them, but the scorn with which they received the apples made my heart sink. I began to think that they wouldn't be willing to feed on any of the foodstuffs that we could give them on the ship.

Eventually, it came to the point where the Red-and-blacks were so sullen and withdrawn, and eating so little, that it was obvious it would have taken months of patient work to adapt them to captivity and to an unnatural diet. To my intense disappointment I decided that we would have to let them go, and this we did. However, as compensation for this, the Black-and-whites continued to thrive and do well, although they would still look with scorn upon anything like apples or bananas. Because the green-stuffs withered so quickly in the heat, they had to be fed four or five times during the day, and this was terribly time-consuming, for we not only had the filming to do but the rest of the collection to look after as well.

It was just about that time that I did one of those stupid things that one is liable to do on any trip. We had been two or three miles down the road into a patch of forest to film a sequence, travelling in the small Land-Rover that the BBC had brought up country with them. When we had finished filming and were returning home, I sat on the tail-board of the Land-Rover and, presently, travelling quite fast, she hit an enormous bump in the road. I was thrown upwards and sideways and landed, fortunately, back on the tail-board, but badly bruising the base of my spine and breaking two ribs. Up till then I had always considered that a broken rib was really not all that painful. I have now changed my views completely. It is *extremely* painful. First of all, I had great difficulty in sitting down, owing to the bruise at the base of my spine; secondly, if I bent down, or even if I breathed, the ribs caused me the most exquisite agony. This made the animal-work even harder because, when cleaning cages, you are forced to bend over quite often, as when carrying buckets of water or doing similar operations. The only pills I had with me were ordinary headache pills which didn't have the slightest effect on the pain. I hoped that after a few days this would wear off. Unfortunately it didn't; if anything, it got worse, and I knew that I wouldn't be able to cope with the collection and the filming that needed to be done on board ship. We needed a third person.

As luck would have it, I knew that Jacquie was getting back to England from the Argentine at roughly the same time as the *Accra* was leaving to come out to West Africa and pick us up. I cabled her and suggested that she came out on the *Accra,* but without telling her why. All this had to be done through Catha at the zoo, of course, because I was not sure of the exact position of Jacquie's ship and so couldn't cable her direct. I presently received a cable in reply saying that Jacquie's ship would arrive at such a time as to give her only forty-eight hours to make all the arrangements to catch the *Accra* at a completely different port. Was it imperative that she join me? I didn't want to cable back the truth of the situation, because I knew that it would worry her, so I merely cabled: 'Jacquie joining me not imperative. Merely that I love my wife.' This had the desired effect of getting her on to the *Accra,* and also caused a certain amount of consternation to the various telegraphists through whose hands it had to pass. Apparently, one isn't supposed to be so out-spoken in cables.

The day eventually came when we had to leave the beef mines and travel down to Freetown. On any collecting trip it is always a difficult decision to try to make as to whether to travel by day or by night to your destination. If you travel by day your animals get terribly hot and the bumpy roads don't enable them to eat. If you travel by night, though you still have the bumpy road to contend with and your animals can't get any sleep, at least they are cool. I decided that we would travel by night. We had to have three lorries, as well as our giant Land-Rover, to transport all the animals that we had collected. The thing that really worried me was the baby animals as they would suffer the most on the journey down to Freetown.

It was at that moment that Sharp came to our rescue. He reappeared in our midst, and immediately offered to drive me with all the baby beef, as we called it, in his small Land-Rover truck down to Freetown – which he could do in a matter of a few hours, whereas the lorries would take all night to do the trip. We could also travel by day in his Land-Rover and stop whenever necessary in order to feed the babies. So, early one morning, Joe Sharp and I left the beef mines with all the baby beef packed into the back of his Land-Rover. Long John was to follow that night with the BBC team and the lorries. As we drove away from the beef mines for the last time I glanced over my shoulder at the sloping range of hills with its beautiful forest. I don't think I have ever been so sorry in all my life to leave a camp site.

Joe drove as rapidly as he could without making it too bumpy for our animal passengers, and we reached Freetown in record time. Here the Diamond Corporation had once more been kind enough to lend us the superb Hollywood flat that we had had at the beginning of the trip, and, moreover, had put at our disposal two large open garages for the animals. I installed the baby beef in the flat and went to bed immediately, for I wanted to be up and about when Long John arrived with the convoy of animals. They were due at six o'clock in the morning, but six o'clock came and there was no sign of the convoy. At quarter past six I began to get a little worried; at half-past six I was even more worried . . . Had one of the lorries run into a ditch and overturned, killing all our precious animals? Or was it just something holding them up, like a puncture? At seven o'clock I was just getting desperate, though there was nothing I could do. Joe and I kept peering out of the windows hopefully, but there was still no sign of the lorries. Then, at about a quarter past seven, the first dusty vehicle lumbered up and drew to a halt in front of the flats. By this time all the other occupants of the flats who knew of the animals' arrival were waiting eagerly on their balconies to get a view of what we had caught. As lorry followed lorry and was parked in the courtyard, their eyes grew rounder and rounder with astonishment. We unpacked all the beef and, to my great relief, I found that none of them seemed to have suffered at all from the journey, except the leopard, Gerda, who was in a slightly worse temper than normal. We stacked them in the garages and then got on with the job of cleaning and feeding them as hurriedly as possible, for I had to go down to the docks to meet Jacquie when she arrived on the *Accra*.

Joe drove me down to the docks, and I took with me a small cardboard box which contained a comfortable bed of cotton-wool and a baby forest squirrel that had just got its eyes open and had been brought in by a hunter at the last moment. These diminutive squirrels are the most enchanting creatures. They have greeny-gold bodies with a white stripe down each side, neat little ears, and a great plume of a tail which is fringed with black on the outside and red in the centre. I knew that Jacquie adored squirrels and it was the only thing I had to take her as a welcoming present. After a certain amount of confusion, because I hadn't realized that you needed a pass, we were eventually allowed through the gate and there was Jacquie standing on the docks, looking mutinous.

'Where have you been?' she said, as a nice, wifely greeting.

'Trying to get on to the bloody docks,' I said.

She came forward to kiss me and I said, 'Don't squeeze me too hard because I've a broken rib.'

'What the hell have you been doing?' she asked belligerently. 'Have you been to see a doctor? Are you strapped up?'

'No, I'm not. I've only just arrived. Here . . . This is a present for you.'

This was an effort to take her mind off my problems. She took the box with the utmost suspicion.

'What is it?' she said, looking at me.

'It's a present,' I said. 'Go on . . . open it. '

She opened it, and immediately forgot all about my broken rib, and everything else, as she crooned over the tiny little scrap of squirrel that lay in the palm of her hand.

'Come on,' I said. 'Let's get back to the flat.'

'It's absolutely sweet. When did you get it?'

'About five minutes before we left, as a matter of fact.

But I took her because I thought you might like her.'

'She's adorable,' she said. 'Have you fed her yet?'

'Yes, it's had its feed,' I said. 'It's all right. You can change its nappies when we get back to the flat. Only, let's get back there, for heaven's sake; there's a lot of work to do.'

'All right,' she said.

'Oh, by the way,' I said, 'this is Joe Sharp. A friend of mine.'

'Hallo, Joe,' she said.

'Hiya,' said Joe.

So, after this demonstrative greeting of a husband and wife who had been parted for some four months, we made our way to the Land-Rover and drove back to the flat.

As soon as we got back to the flat Jacquie installed her squirrel in the bedroom and then said to me,

'Where's the telephone directory?'

'What on earth do you want a telephone directory for?' I inquired.

'I'm going to phone a doctor about that rib of yours.'

'Don't be silly. He can't do anything.'

'He can do something,' she said. 'You're going to see a doctor. I'm not going to do anything else until I've done that.'

'All right,' I said, reluctantly. 'I can go to the flat above. There's a chap called Ian up there. He'll know of a doctor, I suppose.'

So I went up to Ian and got the name and address of a doctor from him, and went down again to the flat. Jacquie was on the phone to the doctor in a few minutes, and explained the situation to him. He very kindly said he'd come round. When he arrived he peered at the large bruise on the base of my spine and told me that I'd probably cracked my tail bone, and then he prodded me vigorously in the ribs so that I leapt about twelve feet in the air with a yelp of pain.

'Ah, yes,' he said. 'I see you've broken two ribs.'

He then proceeded to bandage the whole of my chest very tightly so that I could hardly breathe.

'You are not to bend down, or carry anything heavy, or do anything like that,' he said. 'Not for a while, anyway. By the time you get back to England it should have healed, though. I'll give you some pills that'll take care of the pain.'

The pain-killers worked, and I felt better in consequence, but wearing the bandage tightly wound round me in the heat of Sierra Leone was almost more than I could bear, and in the end I was forced to take it off.

'It's obvious you're not going to be much good on board ship,' said Jacquie, 'if you can't bend and you can't lift heavy things. And if you and John are going to be busy with the filming, that leaves me to look after the entire collection, practically.'

'Oh, we'll manage somehow.'

'Well, I don't think it's very wise,' she said. 'What about getting Ann out?'

Ann, as I have explained, was my secretary, and she had just returned from Argentina with Jacquie.

'Do you think she can get out here quickly enough?' I asked. 'The *Accra* will be back here fairly soon, you know.'

'If we cable her today I think she might be able to get a plane,' said Jacquie.

So we cabled and received a reply almost instantaneously, telling us that she'd got a flight. A couple of days later Ann, a brisk and efficient blonde, arrived and was enchanted by the collection. She'd always had a great love of animals and to help with the cleaning and feeding on board the ship was no chore as far as she was concerned. I explained to her about the Colobus.

'The trouble is that they need finicking with,' I said. 'And, quite honestly, we won't have the time to do it on board ship. I'm not sure how they'll take the new diet, either. So I want to make the entire Colobus group your responsibility and even if you do nothing else, just get the damned things to feed so that we can get them back alive.'

'I'll try,' she said. 'But from what you've told me it doesn't sound as though it's going to be very easy.'

'No, it won't be easy,' I said. 'At least, I don't think so, unless they suddenly go mad over cabbage or something. Anyway, we'll just have to wait and see.'

It was not long after Ann's arrival that we got a new addition to the collection, which proved to be one of the most enchanting of all the animals. As we were having our pre-dinner drinks one evening, the telephone rang and Jacquie answered it.

'It's Ambrose,' she said to me. 'He says he's got a pig for you.'

Ambrose was Major Ambrose Gender of the Sierra Leone Army and I had met him previously when we were in Freetown. He had been introduced to me principally because he appeared on the local television as 'Uncle Ambrose', doing a children's spot in which he always had an animal of some sort to show them and talk to them about. I picked up the phone.

'Hallo, Ambrose,' I said.

'Ah, Gerry!' he said, his deep voice ringing musically. 'I've got you a pig. It's a lovely pig. It's called Blossom.'

'What sort of a pig is it?' I inquired.

'I'm not sure, but I think it's what you call a Red River hog.'

'Good lord! That's marvellous!'

Red River hogs were my favourite of all the pigs. When

adult they're covered with bright, ginger-coloured fur, and they have long tails and great long white plumes on their ears.

'Can you come and collect it?' said Ambrose.

'Yes. Where are you?'

'Well, I'm just going down to the studio to do my spot. Why don't you come down and watch me, and then you can pick up the pig?'

'All right,' I said. 'What's your spot tonight?'

'Oh, I'm showing the Police dogs again. They went down so well last time that we've had letters pouring in asking for a repeat performance. Only this time I'm not going to let them bite me.'

The last time Ambrose had shown the Police dogs he had wrapped a cloth round his arm so that one of the dogs could attack him, which it did, with such vigour that it bit him in the arm, straight through the cloth.

'Right. What time do you want us down at the studio?'

'In about half an hour,' said Ambrose.

'O.K. We'll be there.'

We had a hurried dinner and went down to the studio. It was small but well equipped. The extraordinary part about it was that the great swing doors were never locked when they were on the air, and there was a row of chairs at the back, so that anybody from outside who happened to be passing and wanted to see what was going on in the television studio could simply wander in and sit down. This laxity horrified Chris to the core of his soul.

'It would never work in the BBC,' he said.

'Ah, but this is not the BBC,' said Ambrose. 'This is Sierra Leone Television.'

Ambrose was of medium height and very good-looking, with enormous glistening eyes that always had a sparkle of humour in them. It must have been his military education, undertaken at Sandhurst, that had forced him to grow a magnificent black moustache which he curled up at the ends.

'I'm just about to do my spot,' he said to me. 'So can you wait till afterwards and then I'll give you the pig?'

'All right,' I said. 'I'd like to see you with these Police dogs, anyway.'

Recently, there had been great outbreaks of burglary in the Freetown area, and the Police, in desperation, had imported three trained Police dogs as a deterrent. They certainly seemed to act as one. The three dogs and the three handlers stood there, the dogs panting with the heat of the studio and the lights. Ambrose took up his position in front of the cameras.

'Good evening, children,' he said. 'This is Uncle Ambrose with you once again. Now, we've had so many letters asking to see the Police dogs again, that I've got them on the show for you tonight. First, we will show you how obedient these dogs are. They follow their handlers everywhere.'

The handlers walked solemnly past the camera, the dogs trotting at their heels. They did a circuit and came back and stood in a line.

'Now,' said Ambrose, 'to show you how obedient they are their trainers will tell them to sit where they are, and then the trainers will go to the other side of the studio and you will see how the dogs will obey them.'

The trainers told the dogs to sit, which they did in a panting line, and then walked over to the other side of the studio.

'You see?' said Ambrose, a broad and happy grin on his face. 'Now this dog, here, he's called Peter and he's five years old. This one here is called Thomas and he's four years old . . .'

At this point the third dog, which had got thoroughly

fed up with the whole thing, got up and walked over to the other side of the studio, away from the glare of the lights.

'And that,' continued Ambrose, unperturbed, pointing in the direction in which the dog had disappeared, 'that is Josephine, and she's a bitch.'

I regret to say that our entire party had to stuff handkerchiefs into their mouths to prevent their laughter being heard by the audience.

After a few more demonstrations of how the dogs worked, Ambrose rounded up his little programme and then came over to us, beaming and sweating.

'Now,' he said, 'I can give you Blossom.'

He went over into the corner of the studio and came back with a remarkably small box. I'd been expecting a large crate. He opened the lid of the box and out trotted the most adorable piglet I'd ever seen. She was a dark chocolate-brown in colour, striped longitudinally with bright yellow bands so that she looked like a strange furry wasp of some sort. She had a delightfully snubbed nose, eager bright little eyes, long floppy ears and a long floppy tail. She came out of the box squeaking and grunting with delight, and nosed round our legs eagerly, searching in our turn-ups to see whether she could find anything to eat. We all fell instantly in love with her and carried her back to the flat in triumph. The following day I got a local carpenter to build a proper cage for her.

It was nearly time for us to leave, and I was getting rather worried about how we were going to transport all the animals from the Dicor flats down to the ship. I'd made inquiries in Freetown, but apparently it was very difficult to hire lorries. Ambrose came round for a drink one evening and I happened to mention this to him and asked him if he knew of a lorry firm that could supply us with three lorries for such a short journey.

'What do you want to hire lorries for?' he inquired.

'We've got to get the animals down to the docks somehow. We can't carry them single-handed.'

'But you have the army, my dear fellow,' said Ambrose.

'What do you mean – I have the army?'

'Well, the army, of course. I'll give you three army lorries to take them all down.'

'Ambrose, you can't do that!' I said. 'You can't just commandeer army vehicles to carry animals to and fro to the docks.'

'Why not?' he said. 'I'm a major; I'm in *charge* of the army. Of course I can. What time do you want the lorries here?'

'Well,' I said, 'are you really sure this is all right? I don't want to get you court-martialled or anything.'

'Don't you worry, Gerry,' he said. 'Don't you worry. I'll fix it. Just tell me what time you want the lorries here, and they'll be here.'

So we fixed a time, and sure enough, when the day came the army lorries rolled up to the Dicor flats and the drivers got out and all stood in a line and saluted smartly. It was most impressive. We loaded up the animals carefully and drove down to the docks. Here, they were slung over in great nets on to the ship and down into the hold, while I directed operations as to where each cage should go. The sailors from the ship, and the Chief Officer himself, were exceedingly helpful, but the operation took about an hour and it was in the blazing sun, so it wasn't at all a comfortable occupation. I could only stand by helplessly as I couldn't even lift a crate. However, at last all the animals were neatly stacked in the hold and then we went up on deck and had a last beer, while the ship drew slowly away, and Freetown grew into a mere glimmer in the distance, and the ship's Tannoy blared out 'Rule, Britannia!' over the oily waters.

The first thing that Long John and I did was to go down below and make our mark with the butcher. He is almost the most important man on the ship when you're carrying a cargo of animals, for it is he who has to hard-boil eggs for you or prepare rice, and it is he who is in charge of the cold-room where all your precious foodstuffs are kept. I was a little bit anxious because I hadn't heard whether or not the foodstuffs that I'd ordered had been put on board in England. Fortunately, they were all there: stacks of carrots, crates of beautiful cabbages, apples and pears, and various other delicacies with which I hoped to tempt the Colobus. I told the butcher approximately how much we would need every day, but I warned him that, as the sea air always seemed to have the effect of sharpening the animals' appetites, this order would probably be increased as we went along. He was most helpful and said that he would be glad to do anything to assist us.

The film work that we had to do was quite considerable because the team had not been with us when Long John and I had come out on the *Accra*, and so we had to film sequences of what were to appear as Long John and I on the outward voyage to Freetown, as well as those for the homeward trip. Then we filmed the routine work of looking after the animals down in the hold. There was a fair amount of work that Long John and I could do, but being occupied with the filming the bulk of it had to be done by Ann and Jacquie. Also, I was somewhat restricted in the jobs that I could do because of my wretched ribs. I could feed the leopards, for example, who were now eating chickens and rabbits with a ferocity that had to be seen to be believed. I could stand and chop up food for the other animals, and I also made it my special task to help to feed Blossom.

This was not so much feeding as an all-in wrestling match. We couldn't put her food in the cage because she'd immediately upturn it, and all the fruit and milk and everything would become so sticky and filthy that it would be impossible to clean. So we let her out of her cage to be fed twice a day. She had a large, flat, baking-tin which we piled high with succulent fruit and vegetables, and then filled with milk, and as soon as you sat down in front of her cage and put the tin on the ground, she would start screaming at the top of her voice and banging her little snub nose against the door. This was the tricky part of the operation. You had to open the door and grab her firmly, if you could, to prevent her rushing at the plate, misjudging the distance, and overturning the whole lot, which is what she did on frequent occasions. So, as you opened the door, you tried to grab one of her long floppy ears and hang on to it like grim death, because she came through the door like a bullet out of a gun. Then you'd lead her carefully to the pan and she'd plonk both her stubby front feet into it, little hooves widespread, and dig her nose in and guzzle, uttering purring grunts of satisfaction, and occasionally high-pitched squeaks.

Even when the last drop of milk had disappeared from the pan, and the last crumb of food had been found and eaten, she was still not totally convinced that there wasn't some more to be had if she searched for it, and she would go – if you didn't prevent her – at a mad gallop round the other cages. Normally, she ran round to where the monkeys were, but on one occasion she ran towards the leopards' cage and I only just caught her in time. The cleaning slot at the bottom of the leopards' cage was just wide enough for them to be able to get their paws out, and that might have been the end of Blossom. Blossom, however, as the leopards snarled and clawed at the wire to try and get at her, displayed no signs of fear whatsoever. She gave high-pitched indignant screams, gnashed her little tushes at the leopards and struggled madly in my arms trying to get down and fight them. The leopards were about twenty times her size and yet she seemed absolutely unafraid of them.

Ann, as I had asked her to, devoted herself entirely to the Colobus. As I had anticipated, it was a whole-time job. It was not only a question of getting them used to a completely new series of foods, but also of teaching them new feeding habits. Colobus monkeys have no thumbs. In the wild state they move so rapidly and perform such prodigious leaps through the branches that a thumb would only get in the way, and so these have been reduced to mere knobs. This makes it difficult for a Colobus to pick anything up, because it has to do it with the side of its hand, rather like somebody brushing crumbs off a table. Also, of course, if you are feeding in the top of a tree, you take a mouthful of something and then drop it and it disappears a hundred and fifty feet to the forest floor below; then you move on to the next branch. But in a cage you can't do this. Up country, and in Freetown, where we'd been feeding them on leaves, the matter was fairly simple because we would just push the leaves in through the wire at the top of the cage so that they dangled down and the monkeys could pluck them at their leisure and drop whatever they didn't want. But they would never go down and pick it up off the floor. Now we had no leaves to feed them on, and the nearest approach to leaves that we had was cabbage. This they didn't particularly care for. They also didn't particularly care for any of the other things we had, such as carrots, pears, apples, grapes and so on.

It was a battle between Ann's will to make them live and the monkeys' desire not to eat the food provided, and thus die on us. For hour after hour she would squat in front of the cages, patiently teaching them how to pick things up and trying to get them even just to *sample* a grape or a piece of carrot – just to see what it tasted like – because they would sniff at it and throw it down with disdain without even trying it. The biggest of our Colobus group was an old male who I reckoned must have been some thirteen or fourteen years of age, and we had christened him The Sod because he hated everybody. In particular, he hated Ann. There was a tremendous battle of wills between The Sod and Ann throughout the voyage. If the food was simply put into his cage in a plate he would upset the whole thing and then, to show his disdain for the diet and for Ann, would shuffle himself round and round, backwards, on his behind in the sawdust, so that all the fruit and sawdust got mixed up together in a most indigestible and horrible mess.

Ann had to try another method. Already The Sod hated her with a great loathing which almost seemed to give him his interest in life, and so she would sit patiently in front of his cage holding out food on the palm of her hand. As The Sod could get his arm through the wire of the cage, he would leap at the wire, banging his head against it vigorously, and shoot out his arm in an effort to catch hold of Ann's hand and pull it near enough to the wire to give it a good bite. This would send the food flying across the hold. One day, after this had been going on for some time, Ann decided to try him with a piece of coconut for a change. She thought the white flesh of the coconut would shine more noticeably in her hand, and anyway he'd shown such contempt for most of the other foodstuffs that had been offered to him.

Now, it may have been coincidence but this time, in trying to grab Ann's hand, he grabbed the coconut instead and, pulling his hand back into the cage, sniffed at it before dropping it on the floor. With incredible patience, Ann went on with this performance hour after hour, until at last The Sod began to show signs of wearing down.

He still banged his head on the wire when he saw her, but in snatching at her hand he would grab the coconut, smell it and eat a bit of it. Soon he was taking it from her with considerably more gentleness and it was obvious that we had found something that he really liked. Gradually, both he and all the other Colobus began to understand how to feed from a dish on the floor and they ate a bit more each day. Our spirits rose, for although they were still only eating a small quantity, they were now starting to eat grapes and carrots and bits of apple and, most of all, they were taking their milk which we re-inforced with vitamins. So at least we felt that they were getting enough nourishment to keep them alive. But it was a herculean task and it required all Ann's patience to keep them going. Fortunately, we had no bad weather to contend with, for I think if we had had a heavy sea it might well have made the Colobus seasick. This would have been the last straw, and I'm sure we would have lost them.

At last we got to Las Palmas, rushed ashore and made straight for the local market. Here we purchased everything that we could lay our hands on that we thought might tempt the Colobus, though many of them, of course, were things they'd never seen before: spinach, for example, and strawberries and cherries, and every imaginable kind of green-stuff and fruit that we could use. These we carried in triumph back to the ship and tested out on the Colobus. Needless to say, they turned up their noses at the expensive cherries and strawberries, although they did take to cherries a little later on. The spinach they tried but it didn't seem to satisfy them. However, there was one thing – a strange, bean-like thing – that Ann had spotted at the last moment in the market, and which we'd taken some of just in case. If we'd only known, we'd have brought back a whole sackful, because the Colobus went mad over them and gorged themselves for as long as the supply lasted.

At last we arrived at Liverpool. To my delight, it was a blazing hot summer's day. I thought our troubles were nearly over, for all we had to do now was to get the animals from the ship to the airport and fly them straight across to Jersey. By that evening, I thought, they'd be safely installed and having all the love and care and attention that they could possibly want from the staff. As the ship steamed slowly in to tie up at the docks we were busy down in the hold, nailing sacking and cheap blankets over the fronts of the cages. I always take this precaution, not so much to protect the animal as to prevent people from poking and prying and possibly getting themselves bitten, and frightening the animal in consequence. Also, the animal tends to feel safer in the dark when the cage is being bumped and battered about. Once again they were piled in the great nets, hauled over the side, and put on the docks where the lorries were ready to transport them to the airport and the special charter plane that was waiting for us. We got them all neatly stacked into the lorries and I heaved a sigh of relief. It would only be a matter of a couple of hours now, and we'd be back in Jersey, I thought. Then a small man made his appearance and asked me whether I was Mr Durrell. Beaming happily, I said I was.

'Well, sir,' he said, 'it's about them leopards of yours.'

My heart sank.

'What about them?' I inquired.

'Well, sir, you haven't got any permits for them.'

'But I have,' I said. 'We approached the Ministry, the Ministry passed the permits, and said that as the leopards were only in transit to Jersey they didn't have to be quarantined in England.'

'Well, I haven't got any documents to that effect, sir,' he said.

'Look . . . You've only got to phone up the zoo . . .'

'I don't know about that, sir. If I haven't got the documents, I can't pass them.'

I took a grip on myself. I'd had to deal with petty officialdom so often in the past and I knew that to lose your temper was the worst possible thing you could do.

'Let *me* phone up the zoo, then,' I said.

'All right, sir. But I'm afraid you'll have to pay for the call.'

'I'm quite willing to do that,' I said between my teeth.

We went into his grimy little office and I put through a call to Catha.

Where in hell were the leopard permits? Catha said that she'd just received them herself at the zoo, and thinking this rather peculiar, she'd phoned up the Ministry, though feeling sure that a copy had been sent to Liverpool. No, said the Ministry, kindly, there was no copy sent to Liverpool because they were always sent to the people who were expecting the leopards, or whatever the animals happened to be.

I groaned.

'All right,' I said. 'I'll have to phone up the Ministry, Cath.'

She gave me the appropriate department and telephone number, and I got through to them. They were very apologetic, but the fact was that the permits had been sent to the right place, as far as they were concerned, which was the place that was expecting the leopards.

'Well, will you kindly talk to this gentleman here?' I said. 'He is preventing me from taking the leopards to Jersey because he says he has got no permits . . . Will you assure him that the permits have been issued?'

I passed the phone over to the little man. He mumbled and grumbled and was as obstructive as he possibly could be, but in the end the man at the Ministry convinced him that the permits had been granted for the leopards. He put down the phone rather glumly. It had been the big moment of his day, and I'd spoilt it for him.

'Can I go now?' I said sweetly.

'Yes, I suppose so,' he said, in a disgruntled sort of way.

So we drove out to the airport. But all this had wasted at least an hour of our time and we'd had to phone to tell the plane to stand by. At the airport the animals were all put into the plane and we climbed in after them, sat down in our seats, and fastened our seatbelts. The plane revved up, roared for a moment or so stationary on the tarmac, and then started to take off. Then, suddenly, it stopped. It taxied back again, it revved up again, and once again it started to take off, and then stopped. We taxied back, and this time the engines were switched off altogether. Very apologetically, the pilot came through to see me.

'I'm afraid there's some mechanical fault, sir,' he said. 'We can't take off.'

'How long will it take to repair?' I asked.

'I'm afraid we don't know, sir.'

'Well,' I said, 'can the animals be left in the plane while she's being repaired?'

'We could do that, sir, or we could move them all out and put them in one of the hangars, if you'd prefer that.'

'I think I *would* prefer that,' I said, 'because some of them need to be fed now.'

So all the animals were taken out of the plane again and put in a big spare hangar. Hours passed, and we fed them and gave them all milk. Presently, an official of the airline came to me and said that they were still trying to trace the cause of the trouble, and that they would let me know as soon as there was any hope of us getting off. I phoned Catha up at the zoo and told her what was happening. It came to lunch time, and then it was two o'clock, three o'clock, four o'clock. At five o'clock they came to me and said that they had tested the plane once more, and although they had thought that they had cured the fault, they hadn't.

'It's no good,' I said. 'We'll have to get another charter.'

'Let us have one more try, sir,' they begged.

'All right,' I said. 'But I don't like the idea of going up in a plane that's liable to give out on me. I don't like going up in planes at the best of times, let alone when they're faulty.'

It was quite late in the evening when they came back and said that they had finally fixed the fault. By this time my ribs were giving me hell and I was in a thoroughly jittery mood because, to begin with, I don't like flying, and secondly, the animals were liable to get chilled as the night was growing colder.

'No!' I said, suddenly, with firm resolve. 'I'm damned if I'm going in that plane. I'll get another flight.'

'I can assure you, sir,' said the captain, 'it's perfectly all right.'

'I don't doubt it for a minute,' I said. 'But I just have a feeling, and when I have a feeling I don't fly — which is most of the time . . . I'm damned if I'm going to take up all my animals and myself and my wife in a jinxed plane. No, I'm afraid I'll have to get another charter flight.'

'Well, it's just as you wish, sir,' he said, disappointment in his voice.

So I went to see the airport officials, got their permission to keep the animals in the hangar, and then set about the task of trying to find another charter flight — which wasn't as easy as all that. Eventually we did manage to get one. The following morning we raced down to the airport and peered anxiously into each cage, hoping that the cold night hadn't affected any of the animals. It didn't seem to have done any harm. Then they were loaded into the new plane, and this one actually took off.

When we were airborne, I wiped the sweat from the palms of my hands, lay back, lit a cigarette and closed my eyes. It's almost over, I said to myself; all we have to do is land safely in Jersey. The plane droned on through the sky and eventually the island appeared like a speck on the horizon. We dropped lower and lower and came in to an absolutely perfect landing, and as we taxied towards the airport terminal, there was a row of fork-lift trucks ready to take the cages, and practically – as far as I could see – the entire staff of the zoo.

The animals were unloaded, the press flashlights flared as they took pictures of the leopards and the chimps all the other creatures being loaded on to the fork-lift tr and then taken over to the vans that were to carry the the zoo. Within an hour we were back home, the an had been unloaded, and those that didn't have to un quarantine were released into their new cages. A feeling of relief poured over me. We'd actually go Colobus back. Now we would have ample time to them our full and undivided attention. Now, in addit to their normal diet, we would have an unlimited sup of green leaves to give them – from oak and elm and lin and other such trees, and I felt sure that they would take them and thrive. At least, I hoped it was going to be li that.

8. A Pageant of Births

Dear Mr Durrell,

We have so much enjoyed watching your programme Catch Me A Colobus, *that we would like to send you our congratulations, and best wishes for the future.*

You remind me very much of a friend I had in York about twelve years ago, were you ever called John Mitchell? I should be interested to know . . .

Naturally, when you come back from a trip of any length, you find an enormous backlog of work to catch up with. Although I had been kept informed of the zoo's progress in my absence there were a hundred and one things I had to do. I had to find out what all my committees had been up to, for a start, and I was faced with a desk that was piled almost a foot high in letters that had to be answered. Fortunately, I found that things had been going very well indeed. Our Trust membership had leapt up, so we now had some two thousand, five hundred members dotted about in various parts of the world, and this income, in addition to what the zoo earned from its gate money, would enable us to go ahead with some of our long-cherished plans.

To my infinite relief, all the Sierra Leone animals had settled down very well. The leopards, who were, of course, undergoing six months' quarantine on the zoo's premises, were injected against feline enteritis, to which they took grave exception. And the Colobus, now that they were in more spacious cages which gave them room to leap and to swing, were eating avidly a number of things that they would not take on board ship. We even experimented by giving them bamboo and holly. To our delight they took both of these and ate them very well, so now we knew that we could at least supply them with some green-stuff during the winter months. We had divided them into two groups. The Sod, with the three adult females, was in one cage, and the young male and two females of approximately his own age were kept in a separate cage. We felt it was better to keep the colonies apart because The Sod's temper was never good at the best of times and if we mixed them all together he might do some mortal damage to the young male. As The Sod himself was getting on in years we had no means of knowing how long he would be with us and we did not want our young male, the only other male we had, to be killed or injured.

After the first couple of days, when I was busy in the zoo making sure that all the animals were settling down well and seeing all the new additions that had been done to the cages and so on, I became completely deskbound, answering mail and attending committee meetings. It was, of course, in the middle of one of these committee meetings that Sheena, our adult female chimpanzee, decided to give birth. Sheena had been pregnant for so long that I had almost forgotten about it. The gestation period for a chimpanzee is the same as for a human, and nine months is a long time to wait for a happy event. In the early stages of her pregnancy Sheena had suffered tremendously from retention of liquid which made her hands, feet and face all puffy and, presumably, extremely painful. This is a thing frequently found among pregnant human mothers and so, by consulting our doctor – which we always did, in conjunction with our veterinary surgeons, when the apes had anything wrong with them – we managed to get her to take some pills which reduced this condition considerably. Eventually it disappeared. Apart from the fact that her intake of liquid had increased from two pints to fourteen pints a day, there was no indication that the happy event was imminent. I was in the middle of a Management committee meeting, where we were discussing what new cages needed to be built, what new animals should be acquired, and similar weighty subjects, when suddenly the door of my office burst open unceremoniously and Jacquie rushed in.

'Quick!' she shouted to me, to the astonishment of the assembled company. 'Sheena's going to pop!'

She then disappeared at a run towards the mammal house, and I leapt up, scattering papers in all directions, and followed her. Needless to say, this behaviour completely mystified my poor committee for they did not know that in our zoo parlance to 'pop' meant to give birth, and as I'd never seen a chimpanzee give birth I was determined not to miss it. I raced across the courtyard into the mammal house and skidded to a panting halt in front of Sheena's cage. She was sitting on the shelf with her back towards us, straining, and the very tip of the baby's head could just be seen. Presently, she got up and started building a nest of straw, occasionally pausing to strain slightly but displaying no apparent discomfort. The area of the baby's head that we could see protruding was approximately the area of a goose's egg. She would occasionally reach round behind her and touch the baby's head with her fingers, but she still displayed no real symptoms of distress.

After half an hour of desultory nest-building, with occasional pauses for straining and wandering up and down her platform, Sheena suddenly took up a position facing us, her legs astride, and using only her left hand for support. She seemed, at this point, to be straining with much more vigour, and then – with astonishing rapidity

— she suddenly put her right hand behind her and the next instant had whipped the baby round to the front so that it was lying in the palms of both her hands. This whole action was done so quickly that it would have been almost impossible to photograph. The baby lay back in Sheena's hands, its head lolling slightly to one side. What interested me most was the fact that the expression on Sheena's face was one of absolute incredulity. She had presumably thought that what she was producing was something in the nature of an exceptionally large piece of excreta, and yet, instead of what she had expected, there lay a tiny replica of herself in her cupped hands.

At this point the baby uttered a scream that was so loud and sharp that, if we had not been watching carefully, we would have thought that it had come from Sheena. Sheena's reaction was immediate. She clasped the baby violently to her breast, covering it with both hands. From the moment of birth to this gesture it could not have been more than four or five seconds. For two or three minutes she sat clasping the baby tightly to her like this, and then she gradually loosened her grip and started to examine it. Her first action was to clean the top of the skull by licking and sucking; sometimes the whole top of the cranium would disappear into her mouth, and knowing what large and well-developed teeth she had, I was terrified lest she should suck or bite too hard on the baby's soft skull and thus kill it. But apparently this sucking was very gentle, for the baby didn't seem to be worried by it in the slightest. She then set about cleaning its hands and feet, sucking each toe and finger individually and licking its palms with great thoroughness. Then she held the baby, using her hands as a cradle, and licked its eyes, occasionally stopping and expelling her breath through her pursed lips in what can only be described as a raspberry. Whether this was to spray spittle on to the area she was cleaning, or whether it was an expression of affection, we couldn't really tell. Curiously enough, she evinced no interest at all in cleaning the baby's body. The umbilical cord was long and appeared to be about an inch in diameter and the afterbirth, which was attached to it, must have measured some twelve inches by eight.

Having cleaned the baby, Sheena then, for the first time, became aware of the umbilical cord and the afterbirth and seemed rather worried by them. Holding the baby to her with her left hand she proceeded to walk up and down the shelf holding the cord in her right hand with the afterbirth dangling from it. Periodically, she would put the afterbirth down in the straw, carefully cover it, treading the straw down with her feet, and then retreat and sit down as though she imagined that by this means she had disposed of this irritating object. After a few minutes she would become aware that the baby was still attached to the afterbirth by the cord, and would repeat the whole performance. During the next half-hour she buried the afterbirth under the straw some six or seven times. On one occasion she came to the edge of the shelf and, to our horror, dangled the afterbirth over the side, swinging it to and fro like a pendulum. If she'd dropped it and the cord had broken, the baby might well have bled to death. By this time I'd been joined by my committee and also by our doctor who happened to have been visiting a sick member of the staff. They had watched this performance, fascinated. But when Sheena started swinging the afterbirth over the edge of the shelf, our doctor turned away in horror.

'I simply can't watch it,' he said. 'If she drops it, I dread to think what will happen.'

But, fortunately, Sheena took the weight of the afterbirth in her hand, so it had no effect upon the baby. A little later she got down from the shelf and pulled some straw with her, presumably hoping that this action would rid her of both the cord and the afterbirth, but after a minute she climbed back on to the shelf again.

Within an hour Sheena had become resigned to the cord and the afterbirth as being unwieldy but necessary parts of motherhood, and she then began to investigate the afterbirth more closely, poking it and licking her fingers. Within another half an hour she'd picked it up and begun eating it – but in a rather vague sort of way – more as though she found this was the only way of getting rid of it than as if she enjoyed it. After a time she'd eaten approximately half the afterbirth. She was holding the baby high up on her chest but, as far as we could see, she made no effort to show it where her teats were. This was rather worrying because, in many cases, with a first birth like this, if the mother does not instinctively show the baby where her breasts are, or if she holds the baby too low down so that it cannot reach them, it might well starve to death. However, Sheena was holding it high enough and the baby, mumbling at her body, soon found her breasts. We saw that it was feeding from both the right and left breast. Having fed for a few moments the baby, rather astonishingly, started making chimpanzee greeting noises – the 'eh, eh, eh, eh, eh,' – to which Sheena responded with great excitement, clasping it more firmly to her breast and then peering into its face and licking its eyes at intervals. She went to sleep that night lying on her right side with the baby lying alongside her chest, and we all heaved a sigh of relief that up to this point things were going well.

The following day the umbilical cord was partly dry, as was the afterbirth, but Sheena showed no further signs of eating it. On the third day, the cord, which by now was dry and brittle, broke off, to Sheena's obvious relief. We were well satisfied with the baby's progress; it seemed to be feeding well and Sheena appeared to have plenty of milk. Needless to say, all the mammal staff went about wearing rather smug expressions because, after all, the birth of a chimpanzee is not the easiest thing to achieve in captivity. Indeed, some of the oldest zoos on the Continent – Antwerp, for example, which has been established for a hundred years – had not managed to breed chimpanzees in captivity, so we all felt rather proud of ourselves.

The baby progressed remarkably well and Sheena proved to be a good mother. It was soon crawling about on the floor of the cage and climbing occasionally on the bars, but it only had to utter the slightest sound for Sheena to rush to it and clasp it protectively to her bosom. Muffet, as we called the baby, started to take an interest in fruit at about four months. At first he did not appear to eat it but mumbled it round in his mouth, but soon he started eating it and taking milk from a bottle. It was also when he was about four months old that he was observed playing with straw. He would crawl to different parts of the cage collecting it and piling it in one spot. He did not appear to be bed-making but simply playing. However, after about a fortnight of this activity, he was seen on the shelf, collecting, arranging and stamping the straw into place, and constructing the same sort of nest in miniature that his mother made each night.

Unfortunately, Muffet's good progress did not last. I was watching him closely one day and I decided that I did not like the way he was moving. He was not as brisk and efficient on his hands and feet as he should have been for his age. Also, when he climbed up the wire and started sucking on one of the bars, I noticed that his gums were paler than they should have been. I mentioned this to Jeremy, and he and practically every other member of the staff, as well as Jacquie, all went and peered closely at Muffet. They agreed with me about the paleness of his

gums, but not about his movements. I still insisted that
I thought his movements were curiously laborious for a
chimpanzee of his age. I mentioned this to Tommy Begg
on his next visit and we agreed that we would increase the
quantity of b.12 that Muffet was already getting, to try and
cure his apparently slightly anaemic condition.

As the weeks passed, it became obvious that there was
something very wrong with Muffet, and that we would have
to try to put it right; but we couldn't do anything without
taking him away from Sheena. With the aid of the
Capchur gun we anaesthetized Sheena, went into the cage
when she was unconscious and removed Muffet. Although
we did this as slowly and as gently as possible, it seemed
to be a great shock to him. He was quite used to us, but
he was used to our being the other side of a barrier, and
when we suddenly removed him from the contact of his
mother's body he collapsed. His face and tongue turned
blue and he choked and then stopped breathing. We
tried artificial respiration and the kiss of life, and an

analeptic was injected. This stimulant seemed to have some effect, artificial respiration was applied again and Muffet started to breathe spontaneously. Ten minutes later, however, his heart ceased to beat and breathing stopped. We tried everything we could, but he didn't revive.

Needless to say, we were full of despondency but we sent Muffet's body away for post mortem, hoping that perhaps we could learn from it the reason for his death and that this might help us in the future with any other baby chimps that Sheena might have. The results of the post mortem were very interesting, for it showed the extent to which an animal may be ill without any outward signs of it becoming noticeable for some considerable time. It was found that Muffet's left arm was permanently flexed and the elbow was bound down by a scar tissue, and that the limb bone was not properly calcified. The left hand bottom ribs were distorted and concave. It was also found that he had a massive ulceration near the heart — although there was nothing wrong anatomically with the heart itself — and that this must have caused his death. The post mortem result cheered us slightly as it ended by saying: 'The specimen was definitely extremely stunted and it is doubtful whether this state would have been overcome by treatment even at an early stage of its life.' So at least we knew from this that, first of all, Sheena was obviously not getting enough calcium in her diet, and, secondly, that we were not responsible for Muffet's death as the heart failure would have occurred sooner or later whether we had tried to move him from the cage or not. But this was cold comfort.

However, it was not long before Sheena became pregnant again. This time she gave birth in the middle of the night and the baby was a strong, healthy female which, at the time of writing, is about two years old and is now separated from her mother and doing fine. She shows none of the symptoms that Muffet displayed. Of course, we had increased Sheena's diet in the latter stages of her second pregnancy to allow for the lack of calcium she had had in her milk, and I think we can attribute Alexa's good health to the extra vitamins that we'd been giving to her mother. So at least Muffet's death had taught us something.

It was some time after this that we were cheered up by another happy event. Jeremy arrived in my office in a state of considerable excitement, his nose bright red and his long blond hair flopping in all directions.

'It's the Colobus!' he said. 'They've had a baby!'

Now this was incredible news. There's only one other zoo in the world that possesses this species of Colobus, and as far as we knew they'd never been bred in captivity before. For us, just the fact that we had managed to establish them and keep them alive and healthy was a triumph; if we succeeded in rearing this baby it would be doubly so. We rushed down to the cage to have a look. The three females were all vying with each other in holding the baby which, like all Colobus babies, was pure white at birth, and so it was extremely difficult for us to tell which was the mother. We were not sure what the Colobus behaviour pattern was in the wild state. It was quite likely that they acted like baboons in that, when a baby was born, all the other females took it in turn to play 'auntie' to it. But as the baby was being handed from one to the other and being pulled about so much, we decided that we would have to try and ascertain which was the mother before the baby came to grief.

We went into the cage and managed to get the baby out, whereupon it was hurriedly weighed and sexed. This action proved to us conclusively which was the mother, for the smallest of the three females came down to the wire and made vigorous attempts to get the baby back again. We shut the other two females inside the bedroom and gave the baby back to its mother, keeping her and the baby separate for a couple of days until we felt sure that it was suckling well, and was strong enough to put up with the attention of its aunties. When we reintroduced the rest of the group to the mother and baby there were several minor skirmishes, with the other two females trying for possession of the infant, but when they failed to get hold of it they sat down quiet to groom each other. A few hours later the baby was often seen with the other two females, but as soon as it let out a high-pitched scream the mother would hastily and forcibly retrieve it.

The Sod, who was very much the domineering Victorian father in the group, displayed little interest in his young, constantly brushing it aside and occasionally banishing the female with the young from the inside quarters. Most of the time he completely ignored it, sitting with his normal, superior, faraway look on his face as though he was the lord of all he could survey. The infant progressed very nicely indeed and grew up to be a fine female. We called her Ann, since it was due to Ann Peters' efforts that we'd got the Colobus back to Jersey in the first place. Since then the Colobus have bred again and again, and now we have a group of twelve. As I say, we are the only zoo in the world who have bred them and we consider them to be one of our major achievements.

Not to be outdone by all this activity, Bali, our female orang-utan, became pregnant. This was very exciting from our point of view. It is particularly important that orang-utans should be established in captivity because, at the present rate of slaughter, experts estimate that they might well become extinct in the wild state within the next ten or twenty years. Bali is an exceptionally nice-tempered animal and very placid by nature, and this made our task much easier, for it meant that we could actually go into the cage and examine her periodically. She got bigger and bigger, and it was well past the time that we thought she should have had her baby. We began to get a little worried. As I say, like most of the Continental zoos, we have our doctor to look at the apes in conjunction with our veterinary surgeons because the apes are, after all, so like human beings that a doctor sometimes might be able to make a diagnosis where a veterinary surgeon could be stumped. I was discussing the problem of Bali's pregnancy with Jeremy one day when our doctor called at the zoo on some other matter. We got talking about Bali's baby and I said that I was inclined to think that the whole thing was a myth.

'Well, if I could get my stethoscope on to her stomach,' said Mike, 'it's possible I might be able to hear the baby's heart-beats. Is she tame?'

'Oh, yes,' said Jeremy. 'She's perfectly all right.'

'Well, let's go and have a try,' said Mike.

So we trooped off to the mammal house and Jeremy went into the cage, followed by Mike. He squatted down on his haunches in the straw, put the stethoscope round his neck, and approached Bali slowly and cautiously, talking to her all the time. Bali was lying there looking like a ginger, furry Buddha, and she watched him with her placid almond-shaped eyes in an interested fashion. Eventually, Mike had crawled close enough. He put the stethoscope in his ears and gently started to press the other end against Bali's enormous stomach. Bali was fascinated. Here was this nice, kind gentleman, talking to her so soothingly and pressing something on her tummy which looked as though it might be worth investigating, and which was attached to a long pair of tubes that might even be edible. She gently put out a hand and touched the stethoscope,

but Jeremy made her take her hand away. After a minute or so of listening, Mike took the stethoscope out of his ears.

'Well?' I said anxiously. 'Can you hear anything?'

'Not really,' said Mike. 'There's a sort of double thump which might possible be a baby's heart-beat as well, but she's not exactly lying in the right position. If she was sitting up a bit more it would help.'

Jeremy tried to get Bali to sit up, which Bali had no intention of doing. She liked lying as she was, and was quite happy to lie there and let this strange man poke about at her tummy all day long if it gave him any pleasure. We managed to shift her a little bit to one side, and Mike tried again. Again, he could hear a faint double thump that might or might not have been a baby's heart-beat, but he couldn't be sure. So there we had to leave it. Mike came out of the cage and dusted the straw off his immaculate suit.

'I can't tell definitely,' he said. 'I would have thought that she was pregnant, but really, from the position she was lying in, I couldn't get a conclusive heart-beat. I'm afraid you'll just have to sit it out.'

Which is what we did. Bali continued to grow rounder and rounder, and more and more placid and lethargic. Then, one day, Jeremy went into the mammal house first thing in the morning and, to his great distress, found that Bali had given birth and that the baby was dead. He got it out of the cage and examined it. Our estimate of the length of Bali's pregnancy must have been wrong for the baby, although perfectly formed, was obviously premature and this was one of the reasons why it had been stillborn. But this is not a very uncommon occurrence among first births with wild animals of any sort. What did cheer us up, to a certain extent, was the fact that we had thought that Bali was still too young to breed, and yet she'd had what would have been a very fine, healthy baby. So we kept our fingers crossed and hoped for better luck next time.

I think Bali must have rather enjoyed the extra fuss and attention that was made over her when she was pregnant, because it wasn't long afterwards that she started to display all the symptoms of pregnancy again. Once again she was cosseted; she was separated from her husband; she was given every delicacy we could think off; and, once again, the kind man came and crawled into the cage with her and pressed his stethoscope all over her stomach – without any result. We kept her apart from Oscar until it was well after the time when she should have had the baby if she was going to have it. We decided that this time it was a false pregnancy, which indeed is what it proved to be, because as soon as she was put back with Oscar, her tummy went down and so did her breasts. We were extremely annoyed that she had had us on like that, but we are still hoping that one day she will give birth successfully.

Spring had come again and, once again, the thing that occupied the minds of both Shep and myself, to the exclusion of practically everything else, was the breeding of the White-eared pheasants. The cock bird still had a severe limp and we didn't for a moment think that he would be able to tread the hen. We investigated the possibilities of artificial insemination. Now while this is quite common with domestic birds, little work has been done on it in wild ones, and although we got the most expert advice we could from both the Continent and England, the consensus of opinion was that, as we only had a pair of them and they were such rarities, the risk involved would be too great. We would just have to leave them and hope to goodness that the cock's leg would get better so that one day we might get some eggs from the hen.

About this time I went on my annual holiday to Greece. Of course, whenever I go away it is never entirely a 'holiday', for I generally seize the opportunity to try to write a book during these periods when I'm away from the telephone and other interruptions and can concentrate properly. So I lolled about in the Greek sunshine, enjoying the spring flowers and the olive groves, and then we made our way back, slowly, across France, eating like pigs. Catha and Jeremy kept me informed by letter of what was going on in my absence, and if anything was urgent they always knew where they could telephone me so that I would fly back immediately. But fortunately this wasn't necessary. Jeremy had done a marvellous swap with the Smithsonian Institute in Washington and had got us several different species of Tenrec — strange little hedge-hog-like insecti-

vores from Madagascar which were all on the danger list — and so we were very pleased to have these breeding groups. When we got half-way across France we decided we would telephone Catha to find out how the Tenrecs were getting on and to tell her roughly when we were due to make landfall in Jersey. I was sitting at the dinner table with Jacquie, trying to make up my mind whether I was going to start with *écrevisses flambées* or snails, and sipping meditatively at a nice dry white wine, when the waiter told us that the call we had put through to Jersey had come through.

'I'll take it,' said Jacquie, as she got up and left the table, and I continued my mouth-watering perusal of the menu. Presently she came back and from the exuberant look on her face I could tell immediately that something exciting had happened.

'What's the news?' I said.

'You'll never guess!'

'Well, come on. I don't want to have to muck around guessing. Tell me.'

'It's the White-eareds,' she said. 'They've laid nineteen eggs and Shep's hatched fourteen of them.'

It is difficult to describe the sensations that I felt at that moment. The first was of sheer disbelief; the second a tremendous thrill that ran through my whole body because, if we successfully reared fourteen White-eared pheasants, it would mean that we would have the largest breeding stock known outside China. And if the bird was, indeed, extinct in the wild state, we were now in a position to establish it firmly in captivity and thus save it, as a species, from total extinction. At last the Trust was fulfilling the function for which I had created it. We had a glorious meal and drank far too much wine to celebrate, and the whole of the next day, as we drove through the lovely French countryside, I was thinking to myself: Fourteen of them! Fourteen of them! . . . Sixteen, with the adult pair . . . And if she does as well next year . . . My God! We'll be able to distribute them to all the zoos so that we don't have all our eggs in one basket. I hope to heaven that they don't all turn out to be one sex . . . We'll have to have some special aviaries for them. It's absolutely essential . . .

So, filled with all these exciting thoughts, we reached the coast and crossed over to Jersey. As soon as I got to the zoo I sent for Shep.

'What's all this I hear?' I said, 'about you killing off all the White-eared pheasants?'

'That's right,' he said. 'Whole lot dead. Sorry about it, but there it is. Can't be helped.'

'Come on, you coot,' I said, 'let's go and look at them.'

So he took me up to the special pens where the broody hen was clucking round the pheasant chicks which were by now a week or so old. They were all fine, sturdy, little youngsters and as Shep had taken great precautions to keep them on absolutely clean ground, we felt sure that with luck we could rear the whole lot. I took Shep up to the flat and opened a bottle of champagne, and we solemnly toasted each other and the White-eared pheasants. It was a great moment of triumph for us after all the heart-break and the set-backs that we'd had ever since we'd got the birds.

9. Digging up Popocatepetl

The display is made so much more attractive and beautiful because of the imposing panorama of the mountainous ranges whose hills, in whimsical manner, make up a true marvel of Nature. Added to this, is the warm climate and the flora and fauna of the place.

MEXICAN GUIDE BOOK

One day, when I had finished reading the mail and was skimming through the various periodicals that appear on my desk, my attention was caught by an article in the magazine *Animals* by a Mr Norman Pellam Wright. It was all about a strange little rabbit called the Volcano rabbit or Teporingo. I knew of this rabbit's existence but hadn't realized, until I read the article, that it was in danger of extermination. The Teporingo has a very limited range; it is only found on a few of the volcanoes that surround Mexico City. It is small and quite useless from the point of view of eating, but although it is a strictly protected animal, the local hunters use it for target practice and for training their hunting dogs. Mr Pellam Wright ended his article with a plea that some zoological garden or park should try to obtain some of these little rabbits and establish a breeding colony of them in captivity in case they became extinct in the wild state.

This, I thought, was a job for the Trust. It was an animal we could easily cope with because of its small size, and although I knew that none of the hare or rabbit family were easy to keep in captivity I felt certain that, with a certain amount of patience and perseverance, we would be able to do it. I sat back thoughtfully and pondered on the problems involved. First of all I checked in my reference books and found that there would be a feeding problem rather like the one we had come up against in the case of the Colobus, for the Volcano rabbit lives at a very high altitude in the tall zacaton grass in the pine forests. It appears to feed almost exclusively off this zacaton grass, and I wondered how it would take to other green-stuffs. Secondly, there was the question of altitude. This could be a very great problem indeed, for we would have to fly them out of Mexico to Jersey, and that would mean that they would be coming from something in the neighbourhood of ten thousand feet above sea level to practically sea level itself. Still, I believed that these two problems could be overcome somehow or other.

I thought about the difficulties for quite some time but, meanwhile, there were many other things that I had to do. I couldn't just leap on a boat and go to Mexico at the drop of a hat. I kept the idea in the back of my mind and whilst I was pondering over it I received a letter from Mr Pellam Wright. Curiously enough, I had been on the point of writing to him myself on the subject that was occupying the thoughts of both of us — Volcano rabbits. In his letter he said that he'd heard about the Trust and the work we were trying to do and he felt, if he might be so bold, that the Volcano rabbit ought to be one of our objectives. He assured me that he himself would give every help and assistance he could, should I want to try and catch some. Well, that settled the matter as far as I was concerned. Apart from anything else, Jacquie and I had always been longing for an excuse to go to Mexico and this was the perfect one.

Getting a strictly protected animal from its country of origin is not as easy as it sounds, even for a recognized scientific organization, so both Mr Pellam Wright and I had to undertake a long correspondence with the Mexican Government before, finally, they agreed that I could go and try for Volcano rabbits. After doing a bit of research I had discovered that there were three other species found in Mexico which were in danger of extinction in the wild state, and which were also strictly protected. They were all birds. There was the Quetzal – a beautiful green-gold bird with a scarlet breast and long glittering tail feathers; the Horned Guan – a bird about the size of a turkey with a strange, pointed, rhinoceros-like horn on its forehead; and the Thick-billed parrot – a bright green bird wearing a mask of scarlet feathers across its face and touches of scarlet on its wings and thighs. The Mexican authorities gave me permission to capture the Volcano rabbits and the Thick-billed parrots, but not the Horned Guan or the Quetzals, as they said they were becoming too rare. In any case, they had their own ideas – which they were going to put into operation shortly – for controlling the area in which these birds lived. To get two out of four permits was more than I had expected and I was quite jubilant about the result.

We set about making plans for the trip. Collapsible cages had to be designed and built; various foodstuffs packed; nests made; and, most important of all, we had to find a ship that called at Vera Cruz, the nearest Mexican port to Mexico City, for I knew I would have to go up to the city in order to make my obeisances to the authorities. Eventually we accomplished all this, but it took several months of hard work and a lot of telephone calls and letters. At last we were on board ship and heading towards Mexico.

Our party consisted of Jacqui and myself, Shep – since we were going to collect birds I thought he was the best member of the staff to go, and I like, whenever possible, to take them in rotation anyway — Doreen, my secretary (Ann Peters had left for another job), and Peggy Caird, a very dear friend of ours who had worked for a long time with the BBC and was now free-lancing. I'd asked her to join us as I thought she might get some interesting recordings of the animals so that we could supplement the photographs that we hoped to take of our efforts at catching the Volcano rabbits. I took Doreen along with us because she was a first-class driver, and we would certainly need that in the parts of Mexico we were going to visit, and, anyway, I intended to write another book on the way out.

Four weeks later, the S.S. *Remshied* steamed into Vera Cruz and tied up, and I went up on deck and stared at what could be seen of the town. It seemed gay and alive and warm, and there were pleasant smells in the air, so I decided immediately that I liked Mexico very much indeed. It's unwise to go on first impressions — as I soon found out when we got into the Customs shed. Customs officials all over the world are inclined to be difficult at the best of times and they can be doubly so with an animal collector because he has to take with him such a weird assortment of equipment, ranging from mincing machines to hypodermic syringes, so that they really cannot believe that his sole purpose in coming into the country is to collect animals. They think he must be some highly suspicious sort of travelling salesman. When our mountain of equipment had been spread out along the Customs bench, it stretched for about twenty-five feet and was enough to give any Customs officer pause for thought.

To my astonishment the Customs officer turned out to be a woman, and a handsome one at that. She looked like an enlarged version of Eartha Kitt, and I took to her immediately. In her smart green uniform, and with her beautiful pale brown face, she was a heart-warming sight and

I felt sure that we would get on splendidly together. My heart sank when I saw her scowl at our long line of assorted luggage. It appeared that she was not going to be what I had hoped she would be, which is what they call in South America '*simpatica*'. Fortunately I had Peggy to translate for me because my Spanish is not good enough to go into all the intricacies of why you are collecting animals to a Mexican Customs official. She began, in a rather desultory way, opening our suitcases and poking her hand down the sides. At this rate it seemed to me that we were going to be here for hours and hours — if not for days. Once, in Argentina, I had had all my collecting equipment confiscated by the Customs, and it had taken me weeks to retrieve it so that I could start on the work I had gone to do. I had a horrible suspicion that this was going to be repeated in Mexico. After Eartha Kitt had disputed the contents of the third suitcase (and she still had about another forty to do) she looked at Peggy rather disdainfully.

'Are these all yours?' she inquired.

'Yes,' said Peggy.

The woman thought for a moment, then she beckoned Peggy away to the other end of the counter. Peggy came back, her brown eyes gleaming mischievously.

'She says she wants gratification,' said Peggy.

'Gratification?' I said in amazement. 'What on earth do you mean?'

'Well, she says if we will gratify her she won't bother to look at the rest of the luggage.'

I stared at Peggy in total disbelief.

'But hasn't she got a husband?' I inquired. 'This seems a very strange way of getting luggage through Customs.'

'No, no!' said Peggy, giggling. 'She means a tip of some sort.'

'God in heaven!' I said, shocked, for I'd never attempted in all my life to bribe a Customs official. It's almost like going and spitting in a Chief Constable's eye.

'How much do you think we ought to give her?' I inquired, when I'd recovered from the shock.

'I'll go and see what she wants,' said Peggy, and trotted off to the end of the counter.

Presently she came back.

'She said if we give her three hundred pesos it will be all right,' said Peggy.

'What does that work out to in English money?' I inquired.

'About ten pounds.'

'Oh, well, anything to get the damned stuff cleared.'

I pulled out my wallet and handed the money to Peggy. She went down to the end of the counter where the woman was busy with some other people. I expected the handing-over of the bribe to be done with some circumspection, and so, indeed, did Peggy. She lurked there rather furtively, like some secret service agent who is not quite sure that his disguise is on straight. Eventually the woman noticed her, leant out across the counter over the baggage, and simply held out her hand. Peggy, startled, pressed the money into it and darted back to me.

'Good heavens!' she said. 'So blatant!'

'Well, at least we've got our stuff through,' I said.

We got hold of an ancient gnome of a porter and he took all our luggage, piled it up and said he would arrange for a lorry to pick it up and for it to be taken to a place where it could be stored for a time. For by now I had discovered a new snag. While Peggy and I had been clearing all the equipment, Jacquie and Doreen and Shep had been attending to the paperwork necessary to get our Land-Rover off the ship. I found them in a harassed, sweaty group at the other end of the Customs building.

'Well,' I said cheerfully, 'it's all fixed. All the luggage is through. All done in next to no time . . . marvellous

. . . Best system I've come across in any Customs house in the world.'

'Then you'd better come and try and sort *this* one out,' said Jacquie, acidly. 'Apparently we've got the wrong papers for the Land-Rover.'

'Oh, God,' I groaned. 'Not again.'

The Customs officer was charming, he couldn't have been more polite. At the same time he couldn't have been more firm. He was very much afraid that we had got the wrong papers and that the right papers couldn't be issued there, but could only be issued in Mexico City with the Land-Rover. What did he suggest? He gave one of those expressive Latin shrugs, rather like a duck shaking water off its back. The Señor would have to go up to Mexico City and get the appropriate documents before he could release it. He was sorry, he could do no more. We foregathered in a gloomy cluster and reviewed the situation.

'There's nothing for it,' I said. 'We were going to stay a day in Vera Cruz anyway, so we're booked in at the hotel. We'll have to hire a car, go up to Mexico City and get the right papers.'

'Yes, I suppose so,' said Jacquie. 'But what a waste of time and money. I don't know why the fools at the other end made this mistake over the documents. They knew perfectly well we were only bringing it in for a few months.'

'There's no good arguing about it,' I said. 'Let's get our other luggage into store and get installed in the hotel and we can work from there.'

So that is what we did.

As slight compensation for our frustration, the Hotel Mocambo, lying a little way outside Vera Cruz, proved to be so bizarre and enchanting that it took our minds off our troubles for a brief moment. To begin with, it was enormous and had been designed by an architect who,

I'm sure, was either deeply influenced by Salvador Dali in his youth or else was a frustrated sea captain, because everywhere there were old sailing-ship wheels. Even the entrance hall itself, which was enormous and circular, had a gigantic one hanging from the ceiling. It must have been about twenty-five feet across. All the windows were barred with wheels of sailing ships. Everywhere there were pictures of ships on the walls. The rest of the edifice – and it can be dignified with no lesser term – was a mass of broad staircases leading hither and yon, open balconies that looked down over the trees to the sea, and great patios with Grecian columns that seemed to have been put up haphazardly with no reason at all. I'm sure any professional architect would have gone mad having spent one night in it, but I found it so extraordinary that I was fascinated by it.

We spent the rest of the day organizing a car to take us to Mexico City the following morning, and that evening went down to Vera Cruz in order to sample our first Mexican food. We'd been warned that it was atrocious, so we were more than pleasantly surprised to find that it was anything but. The little Vera Cruz oysters were the sweetest, most delicious oysters I'd ever tasted anywhere in the world, and the great fat prawns, which they split in half and roasted on a flat piece of tin over a fire, were wonderful. They cooked in their own juice and the shells became so crisp that you could eat them as well as the contents of the prawn; it was like eating a sort of strange pink biscuit. Then there were the *tortillas,* which were new to us, a pancake which you could either have in a rather flaccid condition (which I didn't care for) or else fried so that they were thin and crisp like biscuits. With them you ate black beans, and a lovely hot sauce made out of green peppers. We gorged ourselves and began to feel brighter in consequence.

The following morning Jacquie, Peggy and I climbed into the car and drove up to Mexico City, leaving Shep and Doreen to enjoy the flesh-pots of Vera Cruz. The country-side we travelled through was extraordinary and totally unexpected. One minute we were in the sort of tropical zone that lies round Vera Cruz, where you get pine-apples and bananas and various other tropical fruits, and later, as we started to climb, the scenery became totally different; semi-tropical trees and lovely colouring and beautiful shape. Then, quite suddenly, we came to a pine forest zone where the air was cool and we had to put on jerseys. We drove across a great, barren plain and presently could see, looming ahead of us, the Volcanoes Popocatepetl, Ixtacihuatl and Ajusco and, huddling at their feet, a great, grey-white cloud.

'That's Mexico City,' said Peggy.

'What? . . . Do you mean that cloud?' I asked.

'Yes,' she said. 'I was told it was like that. That's smog.'

I looked at her incredulously.

'Do you mean to say that's all *smog*? But they must be suffocating in there.'

'Well,' said Peggy, 'they say they have worse smog than anywhere else in the world.'

'God! It's going to be pleasant staying there for a couple of days.'

We drove through the outskirts of the city which had a rather tatterdemalion air about them, but once we started getting into the city proper the architecture, although mostly modern, was quite handsome. It was true what Peggy had said about the smog: the smell in the air was almost unbearable; diesel fumes, smoke, petrol fumes, and humanity all mixed up together, so that you felt that your lungs would never be the same again. If you got caught in a traffic jam, which we frequently did, you had the choice of rolling up the windows and roasting to death or trying to breathe once every five minutes in an effort to save yourself from catching lung cancer. How people can live and work in Mexico City I just don't know. We booked in at a hotel and then, while Jacquie and Peggy went to try to sort out the Land-Rover problems, I seized the opportunity to phone all the contacts I'd been given, to alert them as to our arrival and what we intended to do. I went round to see Mr Pellam Wright and he was exceedingly kind and helpful and gave me a lot of useful information. He then went with me to see Dr Corzo who is in charge of the conservation of Mexico's fauna, and his second-in-command Dr Morales. I explained to Dr Corzo what I wanted and he readily agreed to everything, although – in spite of pleading with tears in my eyes – he wouldn't agree to let me have a permit for the Horned Guan. Apparently they were going to create a special reserve for it and have it properly patrolled so that no poaching could take place. Although I was disappointed that I couldn't move him on this, at least I felt happy to know that something constructive was being done towards preserving it in the wild state.

The people at the Shell office in Mexico City were extremely helpful to us, and we used their office as a forwarding address for our mail. One day when I went in there the manager, Mr McDonald, happened to catch sight of me as I was inquiring whether there were any letters for us, and called me into his office.

'Tell me,' he said, 'I know you have a party of five, but do you need any extra help at all?'

'Well, I . . . I might . . .' I said, cautiously, thinking that perhaps he had a maiden aunt who had adored animals from childhood and felt she would like to join the expedition. 'Why?'

'There's a young man I know,' he said. 'He's a first-class chap, knows the country inside out, speaks Spanish, naturally, and he's also very keen on animals. At the moment he's waiting to go back to university, but he's got a couple of months on his hands, and I wondered whether he'd be a suitable person for you to take along. He's also got his own car, which might help.'

This sounded extremely promising. We needed a second vehicle and we'd been investigating the possibilities of hiring, but the prices were so astronomical that with our dwindling currency we couldn't afford to indulge in one. If this person had a car of his own it would solve the problem as far as we were concerned.

'What's his name?' I inquired of Mr McDonald.

'Dix Branch,' he said. 'Shall I tell him to come round to the hotel and see you? You needn't take it any further than that if you don't want to.'

'Yes, tell him to come round this evening. Round about five.'

At five o'clock I went down into the foyer of the hotel and found waiting a tall, loose-limbed, well-built young man with long dark hair that had a tendency to flop over his forehead, and rather brooding eyes. I liked him instantly although, after five minutes of conversation, I discovered that he took life very seriously, if not too seriously. I explained what we'd come out to do and asked him what sort of car he had. When he said that it was a Mercedes my spirits rose, and on examining it we found that the boot was so enormous it could take practically half our equipment. I said that as far as I was concerned I would be willing to cover his out-of-pocket expenses if he'd join the expedition to help us with our work. This he agreed to do. From that moment Dix became invaluable. Not only did he know all the highways and byways of Mexico City, the best places to eat, the best shops to get the various things that we needed, but he also had tireless patience in dealing with officialdom, which was something that we needed badly during the later stages of our trip.

Jacquie and Peggy were having no luck with the Land-Rover problem. They were merely being shuffled from office to office and would come back at the end of each day looking thoroughly exhausted and irritable. We had a week of this and then, one day, they came back and found Dix and me sitting in the strange, palm-filled lounge of the hotel, sipping cool drinks. They sank wearily into their chairs.

'We've done it,' said Jacquie.

'Marvellous,' I said. 'But you don't look very jubilant about it.'

'I'm not,' said Jacquie. 'You know what it is? Those fools down in Vera Cruz — it's *their* mistake. It's nothing to do with our papers. The Land-Rover could have come in straight away. They were looking at the wrong numbers.'

Peggy groaned.

'Never do I want to see another government office,' she said.

'Do you mean to say that we can go and get the Land-Rover out?' I asked.

'Yes. It's all fixed,' said Jacquie. 'They phoned through to Vera Cruz and gave them a rocket, I'm glad to say. So we can go back tomorrow.'

As we drove back to Vera Cruz the following morning I outlined my plan to Dix. Although I'd been refused permission to capture the Horned Guan and the Quetzal, at least I wanted to see the sort of country that they inhabited. And so I suggested, as a preliminary, once we'd got the Land-Rover out and our luggage properly sorted, that we drove straight across Mexico and then down to the Guatemalan border, which was the area in which these birds lived. I thought that this would give us a good over-all picture of Mexico and there were many places of interest that we could visit *en route*. Then, when we'd done this, we would come back to Mexico City, make a base there, and work up the volcano slopes after the Volcano rabbit.

We extracted our Land-Rover from the grip of the, by now, suitably servile and apologetic Customs officials, sorted through our luggage in the macabre setting of the Mocambo and left in their custody those items which we thought we would not need. Once we'd done this we were ready and so, at the crack of dawn one morning, we set off to drive right across Mexico to the Pacific coast and then down to the Guatemalan border.

I don't think that anywhere in the world have I travelled through such extraordinarily varied country in such a comparatively short space of time. The first part of our journey took us through the flat lands around Vera Cruz, through sub-tropical creeks and canals where we saw a mass of bird life. There were huge flocks of Boat-tailed Grackles which flew across the road looking like congregations of small black magpies with short heavy beaks. In the creeks and canals, which were thickly over-grown with water-weed of various sorts, were numerous Jacanas or Lily-trotters, those strange little birds with elongated toes that allow them to walk on the water plants lying on the surface of the water. At a casual glance, as they bob their way busily across the water-lilies and other plants that grow so thickly in the canals, you could mistake them for moorhens, but as the cars disturbed them they would fly up and you would see their long trailing toes and catch a glimpse of the buttercup-yellow flash of the underside of their wings as they flapped away to safety. We saw numbers of Boat-billed herons which I think must be the most lugubrious of all the water birds; with their squat, boat-shaped beak and large sorrowful eyes

they sat in clusters in the trees, their strange beaks tucked
into their chests, looking like depressed conventions of
Donald Ducks.

We passed through villages and towns which were a
shimmering blue haze of jacaranda trees and the houses
themselves seemed almost weighed down under the great
shawls of bougainvillaea – purple, pink, orange, yellow and
white. Then, as the road climbed a little higher, we passed
through almost tropical forest where the branches of the
trees sprouted great waterfalls of greeny-grey Spanish
moss, and the trunks of the trees were sometimes almost
completely obscured by orchids and other epiphytes that
grew on them. Here the steep banks of the road were
covered with a tapestry of smaller plants and shrubs and,
in particular, great masses of enormous ferns. The plant life
was so varied and extraordinary that I cursed myself for

not knowing more about botany.

It was while we were travelling through this magnificent country that it began to rain – and rain as it can only rain in the tropics. Great gouts of water plummeted down from the sky so that the road, which was an earth one, was immediately turned into a dangerous mire, and visibility cut down to a few inches. Jacquie, Doreen and Shep were travelling in the Land-Rover, and Peggy and I and Dix were in his Mercedes leading the way. We kept the Land-Rover behind us so that, should the Mercedes – for some reason or other – get into trouble, the Land-Rover could always pull her out. As visibility was cut down to nil by this grey sheet of water that was pouring from the skies, I enlivened the time by reading some extracts from an enchanting guide book that I had been fortunate enough to come across in Mexico City.

'We're not touching in at Acapulco, are we?' I inquired of Dix, for my knowledge of the geography of Mexico was still slightly hazy.

'No,' said Dix, morosely, 'and I wouldn't advise you to go there anyway. It's just a playground.'

'Well, according to this book, it sounds fascinating. Listen to this:

' *"Its particular topography offers impressive panoramas: Quiet and crystalline bays and inlets; beaches worthy of seeing due to the huge waves; the water is warm as well as the climate with soft winds almost the year round* $(77^\circ F)$ *which makes the clothes to wear must be light. It is rare the Sun does not shine, as usually it rains by night. The natives have kept their old customs, specially in dressing."* '

'Wonderful,' said Peggy. 'What a pity we're not going there.'

At this point we had a puncture and Dix and I had to get out and change the wheel, although Dix did most of the work. We got back into the car, dripping wet, and continued at our snail's pace down the road through the torrential rains. When I had mopped the water off my face and hair and hands, I turned once again to my guide book.

'Now *here's* the place we ought to go to,' I said. 'Just listen: *"Due to its temperate climate, its clear sky and shining sun almost all over the year, this place can be considered as ideal for relaxing. The hospitality and friendliness of the inhabitants make the visitor to feel at home, the peaceness of this town is a real soothing for those who are looking for a place to relax their broken nerves because of the excitement of the present way of life almost everywhere. Its parrish and picturesque main square must be visited, as well as its market."* '

Presently the rain stopped and soon afterwards we came to the end of this tropical forest and, in the extraordinary way that vegetation grows in Mexico, passed straight out of tropical forest into pine forest at high altitude. As the sky cleared we drew up to have some coffee that Jacquie had thoughtfully provided. Whereas, some ten minutes previously, we had been sweating gently in the tropical heat, we now found the air so crisp and cold that we were forced to put on all the warm clothing we could find.

Now the road went mad and wriggled its way down into valleys and up precipitous mountainsides and around and along them. The vegetation grew more and more extraordinary as we went along. In the valleys there would be the lushness of the tropics and then a few minutes of climbing up a winding road along a hillside and you would come to a great area in blazing hot sunshine, dry and desiccated, covered with rank after rank of trees that were completely devoid of leaves and whose trunks were of the most beautiful silky-red colour. Both trunks and branches were so twisted that it looked, for mile after mile, as though you were passing through an enormous frozen *corps de ballet*. And then you would round a corner and suddenly there was not a red tree to be seen, but in their place were similar ones, only with a silver-grey bark that gave off an almost metallic gleam where the sun hit it. Again, these were completely leafless.

Round yet another corner and the trees had all disappeared and in their place were gigantic cacti, some of them about twenty feet high. They were the candelabra variety, which meant that they have curving arms sticking out from the main stem so that they look like extraordinary green candlesticks growing thickly all over the mountainside. Here, unidentifiable hawks wheeled in slow circles in the blue sky like little black crosses, and frequently across the road would gallop a Road-runner — a strange little bird with a crest and a long tail and enormous flat feet. When they ran, their feet almost touched their chins, and they leant forward with the earnest air of somebody trying to break the record for the mile. The bird life and the super-abundance of vegetable life made me wish that we could stop more often on the road, but I knew that this would be fatal, for our time in Mexico was short, dictated by the amount of currency reluctantly allowed us by the Bank of England. It was a race against time.

Presently we came to a small town called Tule. To my surprise Dix parked the car carefully alongside the railings of what looked like a little park with a church in it. The Land-Rover drew in immediately behind us.

'What are we stopping here for?' I inquired.

'To see The Tree,' said Dix, in his normal rather gloomy fashion, and giving the tree capital letters. 'Peggy wants to see it.'

'What on earth's The Tree?' I inquired.

'But don't you *know*?' said Peggy excitedly. 'It's the

tree that everyone in Mexico comes to see.'

I glanced at the road. Apart from the three sloe-eyed little girls, in tattered frocks, playing in the dust, there was not a soul in sight.

'It doesn't seem to be over-popular as a tourist attraction,' I said.

'But you *must* come and see it,' said Peggy earnestly.

'Well, in that case, I certainly will,' I said.

We got out of the car and as we did so I heard the sound of weird piping music and the dull thumping of a drum. We went through the gateway into the little park that surrounded the tiny church and there, towering over it, carefully protected by a fence around its base, stood The Tree. It took me aback. It was not only that it was incredibly tall – in fact, I think I have seen taller trees – it was the sheer massiveness of it that took your breath away. A great, towering, whispering pinnacle of leaves, standing on a trunk whose proportions made one gasp; a trunk whose buttress roots thrust out defiantly into the ground, making it look like the foot of some enormous predatory bird, clasping the earth – Sinbad's Roc, perhaps, or something similar. I knew nothing of its history or its age, yet even I, in my ignorance, could see that this was a tree to end all trees. It exuded personality. We were all dazed by it, with the exception of Dix who had seen it before. But even he gazed at it with a sort of reverential awe because he had a great passion for trees.

'They say,' said Peggy, in hushed tones such as one would use in front of a deity, 'they say that it is three thousand years old. It was a big tree – a very big tree – when Cortes came through here, because the population showed it to him.'

I looked at the great fountain of leaves above me and thought that, in that case, it must have been already a young sapling a thousand years before the birth of Christ.

The only other people who were there were an elderly, blind Indian clad in tattered, faded clothing and a battered straw hat, who was playing on a flute – a strange, uncanny, almost oriental tune – and standing beside him a little boy of six or seven who was beating out a complicated tattoo on a drum. They took no notice of us whatsoever.

'What do you think they are doing?' asked Peggy, since they hadn't turned their attention on us and were therefore, presumably, not seeking to earn a few pesos by playing to us.

'I bet you he's playing to the tree,' said Jacquie.

'Good God! He might be,' I said. 'Go on, Peggy, go and ask him.'

'Well, I don't really like to interrupt him,' said Peggy, who tended to get shy at moments of this sort.

But at that moment came the opportunity, for the man took the flute from his lips and wiped his mouth and just stood there facing the tree, and the boy ceased his drumming and stood looking at the ground and shuffling his bare toes in the dust.

'Go on . . . Go and ask him now,' I said.

Rather timidly, Peggy went over and we heard her speaking to the man. She came back, her face alight with delight.

'He *is* playing to the tree,' she said. 'He *is* playing to the tree!'

'There you are,' said Jacquie triumphantly. 'I knew it!'

'But what's he playing to the tree for?' I asked.

'I didn't like to ask him that,' said Peggy. 'I felt it would be rather . . . rude, somehow.'

'Well, I think you ought to get a recording of him,' I said.

Peggy got her recording equipment out of the car and when the man next put the flute up to his lips, turned his blind eyes to the tree and started playing, she recorded the whole thing.

Was he, I wondered, playing to the tree in the hope that it would restore his sight to him? Or just because it was the tree to end all trees? We none of us felt like asking him, and presently we walked out of the little garden and got back into the cars. As we drove away we could still hear the plaintive noise of the blind man's flute and the rat-a-tat-tat of the little boy's drum as they played to the giant tree.

Our trip towards the Guatemalan border, in order to try and see the Horned Guan and the Quetzal, was completely abortive, though the trip itself was fascinating. We ended up in the village of San Cristóbal and from there we could go no farther because at that time there was some political upheaval going on in Guatemala and guerrilla forces were dodging to and fro across the border. We were warned that, should such a rich-looking party venture any farther, we might run into one of these bands of guerrillas, in which case they would undoubtedly shoot us out of hand for the sake of our equipment and clothing and any money we had with us. With the utmost reluctance, we turned back and headed once again for Mexico City.

When we got back to the city we decided that it would

be cheaper for us to live in a flat and through the good
offices of a friend in Shell we did manage to find one that
was ideal. It was centrally situated, it had three double
bedrooms, two bathrooms, an enormous living-room and a
kitchen. Once installed in this we went our various ways, for
the female members of the party wanted to do shopping and
sight-seeing, while Dix and Shep and myself were going to
go on rabbit hunts.

I decided that our first attempt should be on Popocatepetl
itself and so, very early one morning, we piled all our
equipment into the car and drove off towards the giant volcano. As we climbed higher and higher and it became
colder we looked back. In the pale dawn light, in the great
bowl formed by the ring of volcanoes, we could see the
patchwork quilt of Mexico City, a glitter of coloured
lights – for at that hour of the morning the smoke had not
built up. By afternoon, from the same vantage point, you
wouldn't have been able to see the city at all.

At the base of Popocatepetl there were several little
hotels. We chose the least scruffy-looking and established
ourselves there. The owner of the hotel was a loquacious,
crafty Mexican. We asked him about Volcano rabbits,
since he was a keen hunter and possessed a couple of
hunting dogs. He told us that the Volcano rabbit was found
right up as far as the edge of the snow-line on the volcano, and that he would try to contact a friend of his whom
he thought might be able to help us. While we were waiting for this friend to materialize we drove up the
volcano as far as the road allowed, into the Popocatepetl
National Park, for I felt that, if we talked to the park
rangers, they would be sure to be able to give us information about the whereabouts of the Teporingoes. The road
zigzagged up the volcano and presently we were driving
through thick pine forest. Underneath it grew the zacaton
grass in great golden clumps like enormous uncombed

wigs. When we eventually got to the park and out of the cars, the atmosphere was beautiful, the air so sharp and clean that it almost hurt your lungs to breathe. Above us towered the enormous dome of snow that was the top of the volcano. We had some difficulty in finding a forest guard but eventually, when we did find one, he became quite eloquent about Volcano rabbits. Yes, he knew them, and had seen them quite frequently in different parts of the park and on the other slopes of the volcano. In fact, he had actually caught a couple, he said proudly.

'Where,' I inquired, 'are they?'

'Oh,' he said, 'I ate them.'

This is an animal which, on paper at least, is one of the most strictly protected creatures in Mexico, and this was a forest guard, inside a national park, speaking to me. This sort of thing is not just common to Mexico, it is common all over the world where animals receive what I call 'paper protection' but are not protected in fact.

Having established that at least there were, in spite of the guard's efforts, some Teporingoes left, we returned to the hotel where we found that the owner had run his friend to earth and brought him round to see us. He was an enormous, well-built man, with a great slab of a face, rather like one of the more unattractive Mayan carvings, and he had quick, shifty eyes that seemed almost too small for his face. But he certainly seemed knowledgeable about the whereabouts and habits of the Volcano rabbits. The only way to catch them, he told us, would be to dig them out. This was a laborious process, but he suggested that, with two other men and himself and Dix and Shep and myself, we should be able to do the job. So we arranged to go up the volcano once again the following morning and start on our first rabbit hunt.

I had read up all I could about the Volcano rabbit and its habits – which was precious little because nobody seemed to have studied it to any great extent – and we knew that they lived only in the zacaton grass and fed almost exclusively on it. One authority does say that they feed on an aromatic wild mint that grows up there, but we could never even find this herb, let alone catch a rabbit feasting on it. The zacaton grass, we soon discovered, is not the easiest sort of place to hunt for anything. It is tall – as much as three feet high – a very pale golden-yellow in colour, and it grows in huge tussocks all over the soft, black, volcanic soil.

In this soil the Volcano rabbits dig long and complicated burrows. Under the overhanging zacaton they work out a network of little runways, almost like tunnels, and they seemed to browse on top of the zacaton tussocks, feeding on both the new and the old grass, for a number of tussocks we found had been chewed as flat as a mown lawn on top, only leaving a sort of rim of overhanging grass round the edges. We drove up the slopes of Popocatepetl to about ten thousand feet, slowly, keeping a sharp look-out in every direction for any sign of a Volcano rabbit. I didn't really think that we had any hope whatsoever of seeing one, for I felt sure that the noise of the car would send them diving for their burrows. But then we rounded a corner, and there to my complete astonishment, sitting like a sentinel on top of a large clump of zacaton, was a Teporingo.

In spite of the fact that we skidded noisily to a halt, the Teporingo, in a well-bred way, continued to sit on his clump of zacaton and ignore us completely. Although he was only some thirty feet away I examined him minutely and avidly through my field-glasses. He was approximately as big as the domestic rabbit known as a Netherland Dwarf – that is to say about the size of a fairly plump guinea-pig. His small, neatly-rounded ears were pressed close to his skull so that you had to look carefully to notice them at all, and there was absolutely no tail visible. His colour-

ing was predominantly brown with a tiny white ring round the eyes which set it off, and his pelage had a sort of greenish tinge to it where the sun struck it. Having assured myself that it really was the animal that I'd come so far to find, and not one of the other species of rabbit that inhabit Mexico, we all vacated the car in a body. At this the Teporingo gave a slight squeak, like somebody rubbing a damp thumb over a balloon – but more piercing – jumped vertically into the air, landed once again on the tuft of grass he'd been sitting on and, using it as a sort of springboard, dived into the zacaton and disappeared.

Immediately we set to work. We rigged up a net round the entire area and then searched under the zacaton clumps to block up any exit holes that we thought his burrow might have. Having done this we concentrated our attention on the burrow down which we thought he'd disappeared, and started to dig. Dix, Shep and I were unaccustomed to this altitude and we found that the smallest action made us gasp for breath. Even the setting up of the nets, which was a simple enough operation in itself, left us gasping and wheezing like ancient cart-horses on their way to the knacker's yard. So when it came to the digging we found it exhausting, to say the least, and after a time just had to sit down and leave the operation to our three hunters. They didn't mind in the least and dug away with great vigour, apparently unaffected by the altitude. They dug and dug and produced a mountain of soft, almost powder-like black volcanic earth as they excavated the burrow: but there was no Teporingo. It was obvious that there was some side passage which we had not discovered and had left unblocked, and he had escaped. I was bitterly disappointed and could see that catching Volcano rabbits by this method was not going to be at all easy. However, we moved farther along the slope of Popocatepetl and when we found an area which we knew to be inhabited by the rabbits, we set to work again.

First we searched for a burrow that had fresh droppings outside so that we were reasonably sure it had an occupant before we started to dig. Then again we went through the laborious process of blocking up every other hole we could find in the vicinity, and digging commenced once more. Five times we did this and five times we met with no success. Then, at last, on the sixth dig we were lucky. One of the hunters who had been digging suddenly gave a small inarticulate grunt, got down on his knees in the black soil, thrust his hands into what was left of the burrow they were excavating, and pulled out a young, bright-eyed, and very much alive Volcano rabbit. After one preliminary wriggle it made no movement at all but just lay in his hands. Fearing that it might be suffering from shock, we hastily sexed it, found it was female, and transported it with the utmost tenderness to one of the cages that we had brought with us.

Knowing that both rabbits and hares, when they are put in captivity, show an extreme tendency to nerves and can easily kill themselves by jumping straight at wood or wire if what they consider an enemy is too close, I was a little frightened that this, our first Teporingo, might do the same when put into the cage. I had a coat ready to put over it so as to make her feel safer. But when we put her in the cage she simply sat there, placidly staring at us. After a moment or so I tentatively put out my hand and scratched gently against the wire to see what effect it would have. I was quite taken aback when the Teporingo gave a tiny hop, came over to the wire and smelt my finger. It was as though we had captured a domestic animal instead of a wild one, she seemed so tame and phlegmatic about the whole thing.

It was growing towards evening now and the great snow-cap of Popocatepetl was turning a delicate shade of pink in the falling sun. I decided, when I'd finished gloating over our capture, that the best thing would be to take her back straightaway to Mexico City and see how she settled down before progressing any farther. This we did, and on the drive back to the city I gave the subject of Volcano rabbits and their capture some attention. It was obvious that if we were going to pursue them at such heights the three of us were useless as hunters because of the altitude, but I knew that they did exist in little pockets farther down the flanks of the great volcano. It seemed to me that the sensible thing to do would be to choose several villages that lay along the base of Popocatepetl and use the method that I'd employed in many parts of the world before, which was to alert the villagers and offer a reasonable price for any Teporingoes brought in unharmed. However, before we did this, I wanted to make sure that the Teporingo we had caught was going to settle down and adapt itself to captivity. It was one thing to

catch your animal, I reflected, thinking of past bitter ex-
periences, and quite another thing to keep it.

When we got back to the flat in the city the Teporingo,
in her wire cage, was placed reverently on a large sheet of
newspaper in the middle of the living-room floor, and we
then sallied forth to a local market where we purchased
as many different kinds of fruit and vegetable, green-
stuffs and herbs, as we could lay our hands on. When
we got back to the flat the Teporingo still seemed as unperturbed as she had been the moment she was caught. We
carefully prepared the food and counted it – so many
sprigs of this, so many sprigs of that, so many pieces
of apple, and so on, so that we could tell exactly what had
been put into her cage and what, if anything, she was
going to eat and show a preference for. Then we placed
these delicacies in the cage, covered her over so that the
cage was partially dark and would give her a greater sense
of security, and went out.

We had a very good dinner to celebrate and when, some
three hours later, we came back, I cautiously removed
the covering from the cage to see if she'd eaten something.
I didn't expect for a moment that she had, because it
generally takes a wild-caught animal a certain length of
time to settle down, and I knew that the food was completely new to her. So I felt slightly incredulous when
I found that she'd eaten nearly everything in the cage
with the exception of one herb which apparently was not to
her liking. She'd even eaten the apple, which I didn't
think she'd touch. While delighted with this response I
knew that we would still have to wait a few days to
make sure that the new diet was not going to affect her
in any way and produce enteritis or some similar malady
which might easily kill her. But it was a first class start;
almost too good to be true.

The following day, leaving our first Teporingo in

Jacquie's care, Dix and Shep and I investigated the villages that lay along the lower slopes of Popocatepetl. There were quite a number of them but only two had what we considered to be Teporingo colonies within easy striking distance. We interviewed the equivalent of the mayor of each village, told him what we wanted and offered what was, for the poverty-stricken Mexican, a very high price for any Teporingo brought in unharmed. We left them with a suitable supply of cages and promised that we would come back in two days' time to see if they had achieved any results.

For two days I watched our rabbit like a hawk for any sign of distress or disturbance, but she remained placid and, with the air of a gourmet, ate practically everything that we put into her cage. I hoped fervently that the two villages we had been to had been successful, because our time in Mexico was growing short and, although we had achieved what we had come out to do, one solitary female was of no earthly use. What we wanted was the full complement allowed by my permit, ten in all, of which I hoped at least four would be males. In this way we could set up a colony with some hopes of breeding.

Now that I appreciated the difficulty of obtaining the Teporingoes I had, mentally as it were, scratched off the list the other species which I had permission to capture but which I didn't think we'd have time to acquire. That was the Thick-billed parrot. But during the two days we were waiting before we went back to the villages to see whether they had caught any Teporingoes or not, we had an extraordinary piece of luck. I had been told about an animal dealer whose establishment was on the outskirts of the city, and although I knew that the animal dealers were carefully controlled by the Ministry and were not allowed to handle any strictly protected animal, I thought it would be worth going down to see what he'd got.

When we arrived, to my delight, there was a cage with three pairs of Thick-billed parrots clambering about, gaudy, raucous, with a glint of mischief in their eyes and not a feather out of place. After some protracted bargaining I purchased all three pairs and we carried them in triumph back to the flat. They were beautiful young birds in perfect condition and Shep went into ecstasies over them. Although they were delightful and colourful and I was pleased to have got them so effortlessly, I still concentrated mainly on the problem of the Volcano rabbit. Having obtained one, it would be a bitter blow if we could get no more before we were due to leave and I knew that, should we not be able to obtain any more, we would have to take this female and release her again where we had caught her, thus defeating the whole object of the expedition.

The days passed, and at regular intervals we visited the two villages. They assured us that they had dug and dug with no success — which I could well believe. All I could do was to raise the price we were willing to pay for the rabbits to an astronomical degree, in the hopes that this would give them the incentive to go on trying no matter how often they failed. But each time we came away from the villages empty-handed I felt more and more depressed.

And then, one day, our luck seemed to change. We went on our routine call to the villages and in the one called Parras, as soon as we drew up in the dusty main street opposite the mayor's house, we could tell from the way he rushed out beaming and waving to us, that they had had success. He led us through his house and out into his tiny back-yard and there, in the cages that we had left with him, were three Teporingoes. They were all unharmed, sitting placidly in the cages and seeming as phlegmatic about their capture as the original one. Carefully we lifted them out and sexed them, and my spirits dropped slightly, because all proved to be female. Nevertheless, four Teporingoes were better than none, so we paid the triumphant mayor for the rabbits and took them back to the flat. As an experiment we tried putting two in one cage, but we soon found that they were of a pugnacious disposition and had to keep them all caged separately.

The new rabbits took to the strange diet that we had to give them as easily as the first one, and this was a hopeful sign. The one thing that really worried me was that

our time was running out. We had only a few days left
before Shep was due to fly back to Jersey with whatever
we had managed to acquire, and the one thing that we
didn't have was our full quota of Volcano rabbits. Most
important of all, we still had no male. A couple of days
after Shep's departure the rest of us were due to make
our way down to Vera Cruz to board the ship, so there
would be no time left for us to catch more Volcano rabbits.
We went out to the villages every day now, inciting them
to further efforts and raising the price to a ridiculous
sum but, although they obviously were working hard at
it, no more Teporingoes were forthcoming. In desperation,
I felt that there was only one thing to be done. Taking
Dix with me to act as translator I went back to see Dr
Morales of the Ministry of Agriculture, and explained my
predicament. I pointed out that, having travelled so far
and spent so much money trying to obtain the Volcano
rabbits, to take only four – and all of them females – back
to Jersey was futile to say the least. If he would allow my
permit to be re-issued in Dix's name, Dix could then
try and obtain six more Teporingoes after I'd left. Among
those I was fairly certain there would be some males.
To my relief, Dr Morales was most sympathetic. He saw
my point, and immediately agreed to transfer my permit to
Dix, for which I was most grateful.

The next twenty-four hours were a tremendous rush.
Special travelling cages had to be built for the Teporingoes,
and a special cage for the Thick-billed parrots – one that
would not only be suitably light for air travel but which
would be indestructible – for the parrots had formidably
large beaks and could demolish anything made out of plain
wood in a quarter of an hour or so, and I had no desire to
have them loose in a plane flying across the Atlantic.

The day came when Shep had to leave with his precious
cargo, and we went down to the airport to see him off.

He promised me that he would get Catha to phone me a couple of days after his arrival to let me know how our four Volcano rabbits were faring. We had found that it was simpler to communicate with the Trust by telephone than by cable because the cable came out at the other end in such a garbled form that whoever you'd sent it to was forced to reply by asking you what you'd said in the first place. By the time this had gone on for two or three cables it became infinitely cheaper to telephone.

A couple of days later Catha phoned me. She told me that the Volcano rabbits, the parrots, and Shep, had all arrived intact. The rabbits had settled down, as had the parrots, and there was nothing to worry about. This was a tremendous relief, but the next thing was that Dix should procure some more Teporingoes for us, among which would be a male. I briefed him on this job so often that I must have become a bore. I impressed upon him that he must sex carefully all the rabbits that might be caught and, although he could accept another three females, after that – if any females were caught – he must let them go and keep trying until he got a sufficient number of males to make up the complement on the permit. He knew how to feed and look after them and how to cage them for the journey, so I was not worried on that score, and I knew that his natural love of animals and his sensitivity would make him look after them properly. Having tied up all the loose ends, we made our way back to Vera Cruz and got on board the ship. It had been a fascinating but also a frustrating trip. If Dix could pull off the final thing and get us a male Teporingo I felt that the whole expedition would have been a success, but I could only wait with my fingers crossed and hope for the best.

On our arrival in Jersey one of the first things I did was to make a bee-line for the Teporingoes to make sure they were all right. I learnt from Gill, the girl who had been looking after them, that nineteen days after their arrival the oldest female had given birth to twins and that for forty-four hours everything seemed to be going all right. Then the babies were found dead in the nest. I think this must have been caused by inadequate attention on the part of the mother. She had, after all, been caught when she was pregnant, transported from a high altitude to a smog-ridden city, taken by air to Jersey and a very low altitude, and had not really got accustomed to her surroundings before she had been faced with the problem of bringing up two babies. It was disappointing from our point of view but you could hardly blame the mother.

Weeks passed and there was still no word from Dix. I kept writing him encouraging letters, urging him on, to which he didn't bother to reply and I began to have a feeling that, having worked so hard and tirelessly with us on the trip, he'd grown dispirited with the whole idea of Volcano rabbits. Then, one morning, the telephone rang. Was I prepared to take a telephone call from Mexico? I couldn't tell the operator how eagerly I'd been awaiting this call, so I merely said 'Yes' in a flat voice. Dix came on, and it was one of those miraculous lines where his voice was as clear as a bell, almost as though he'd been in the room speaking to me. He told me that he'd succeeded at last in getting six more rabbits, two of which were males, and that they'd settled down in his house and were feeding well. He'd just completed constructing the travelling boxes for them, and he'd be sending them off within the next twenty-four hours. I got from him the flight number of the plane from Mexico and all the other details. I was wildly excited. When you go on an expedition you can't always guarantee success, but so far, on all my expeditions, I'd had incredible luck. It seemed that now the Mexican expedition was not going to be a failure either. As soon as Dix was off the line I contacted London Airport. I spoke

to every official I could think of on the subject of Volcano rabbits; I stressed their rarity and the importance
of their being sent to the Animal Shelter should they arrive
too late to catch a connection to Jersey; I phoned up Mr
Whittaker at the Animal Shelter itself, which is run by
the RSPCA, told him the glad tidings, and gave him
minute details as to what to do should they have to be
in his care overnight. There was nothing more I could do
except sit back with ill-concealed excitement and wait for
their arrival.

We had worked out that their flight would arrive in
the morning, which would give plenty of time for them
to be put on another plane to Jersey, and when the great
day dawned I waited impatiently for some news. Two
hours after the plane must have touched down at London
Airport I phoned to see what was happening. None of the
officials knew anything about Volcano rabbits. I got on to
Mr Whittaker. No, he'd not received the rabbits, although
he had everything prepared for them. At lunchtime
I phoned again, and still the officials denied all knowledge
of Volcano rabbits. By this time I was getting a little desperate and was wondering whether I should put in a phone
call to Dix to find out whether he had, in fact, succeeded
in getting them off on that particular flight. At four
o'clock that afternoon I phoned London Airport again.
Again they denied all knowledge of the rabbits.

Once again I got on to Mr Whittaker and told him that
I was exceedingly worried. He said that nobody had been
in touch with him about any livestock on the airport, but
that he would investigate and phone me back. Eventually
he told me that he had tracked the rabbits down, and they
were now in his care. Apparently, there had been some
small discrepancy in the papers so necessary for the petty
civil servant, and the rabbits had been pushed into a

hangar somewhere and left while the vital work of fixing their papers had gone on. Mr Whittaker assured me that he'd had a look at them and, although obviously frightened, they all seemed in good health. It was too late that day for him to get them on a plane to Jersey so he had to keep them overnight and fly them across to us the following morning.

When the cage arrived at the zoo we tore the sacking from the front as gently as our eagerness allowed and peered in. There were five rabbits alive, looking somewhat startled. The sixth was dead. Carefully, we unpacked them and sexed them. The dead one, needless to say, was a male. Among the other five was one male and four females. To say that I was angry would be putting it mildly. I felt that the quite unnecessary delay at London Airport had deprived us of this male. Our new arrivals were put in cages separate from the ones that we had already got, to await all the tests that were so necessary before we could introduce them.

I paced up and down the office and wondered what was the best way of blasting London Airport out of existence. Suddenly I had an idea. Sir Giles and Lady Guthrie were members of the Trust, took a deep interest in our work and had helped us on many occasions. Sir Giles was the Chairman of BOAC. If he couldn't scald somebody's tail for them, nobody could. I picked up the telephone and asked for his number. It turned out he was away in Switzerland but Lady Guthrie answered. I told her the tale of the Volcano rabbits and I explained that the only reason I wanted to make a fuss was that should other rare creatures be consigned to us at some future date, and for some reason or other they had to spend some time at London Airport, I didn't want the same sort of thing to happen.

'Of course not,' she said briskly. 'Absolutely ludicrous! I'll see to it myself. As soon as Giles gets back I'll get him on to it.'

And this is exactly what she did. Over the course of the next week or so I got letters of abject apology from various officials at London Airport, making innumerable excuses for the bad handling of the rabbits. These were satisfying in that I knew in future anything consigned to us would automatically light up a red warning light in the minds of officials. But no amount of apologies would bring back to life our male Teporingo.

What we did now was examine the females at regular intervals and when we found they were in oestrus we would introduce the male into the cage for a few hours and keep a careful watch. This was necessary because, as I said before, the Teporingoes were highly pugnacious, and we didn't want to run the risk of the last male being killed by one of the females. This went on for some time and then, one day, we found that one of the females had built herself, in her bedroom, a neat nest of straw lined with fur from her own body. In it were two babies. This was, of course, a terrific thrill for us. We watched the babies' progress day by day, and as they grew bigger and bigger we felt more and more swollen-headed. But perhaps we became a little too proud of our achievement for, as often seems to happen on these occasions, fate dealt us a couple of nasty blows. Firstly, Gill went down one morning and found that, in some inexplicable way, one of the baby rabbits had managed to strangle itself with a hawthorn branch, getting it wound round its neck and jammed in the wire. This left us with just one female baby. The next thing was that our male died. The post mortem showed that he'd died from coccidiosis which is one of those diseases very difficult to diagnose in the early stages.

Immediately all the remaining rabbits were given 'Sulphamezathine' as a preventative against them catching it – for all of them, at one time or another, had been mixed with the male, but, in spite of this, we lost two females in the same way.

We were now, it seemed, back to square one. We had a lot of females and no male. However, at this time we had just prepared and published our fifth Annual Report in which there was a full account of the Mexican expedition, together with photographs of the female rabbit with her baby. I sent copies of this to both Dr Corzo and Dr Morales and, of course, to Dix Branch, and at the same time I wrote to Dix and asked him if he'd be willing to undertake a rabbit hunt on his own, should I be able to get permission from the Mexican government for some more rabbits to be captured. He wrote back enthusiastically, saying that he would do everything possible to help. I sat down and wrote to Dr Morales explaining our predicament. I said that, although we had a group of females which we couldn't turn into a breeding group because there was no male, we had at least proved a number of things and that therefore our efforts had not been entirely in vain. For example, we'd proved that the Volcano rabbit could be kept in captivity and, moreover, kept at a much lower altitude than it was used to, and that it could be bred in captivity. We'd also found out a number of interesting pathological things about it, including the fact that the particular 'brand' – if you like to call it that – of coccidiosis that it was suffering from might be a brand peculiar to that animal. And we had worked out the gestation period which hitherto had been in doubt. In view of our success rather than our failure I asked Dr Morales whether it would be possible to issue Dix Branch with a permit to try for some more Volcano rabbits for us. To my great delight he wrote back the most charming letter saying that, as we had been so successful, he would most definitely grant Dix a permit to capture some more rabbits. I hope that this will come to pass shortly, and that this time we will have greater luck and establish a colony of these rare and attractive little creatures in the Trust's collection.

When man continues to destroy nature, he saws off the very branch on which he sits since the rational protection of nature is at the same time the protection of mankind.

EXTINCT AND VANISHING ANIMALS

On the bookshelves that line my office there are two squat, fat, red books that glower at me continuously. They are the first things that catch my eye in the morning and the last things that catch my eye as I close the office door at night. They act as a constant reminder. These are the Red Data Books produced by the International Union for the Conservation of Nature. One deals with mammals, the other with birds, and they list the mammals and birds in the world today that are faced with extinction – in most cases directly or indirectly through the interference of mankind. As yet there are only these two volumes, but there are more to come, and they will make a depressing line when they eventually arrive, for there is a further one on reptiles and amphibians, another on fishes, and yet another on trees and plants and shrubs.

I was once interviewed by a reporter from some newspaper or other, who said:

'Tell me, Mr Durrell, how many species of animals are actually endangered?'

I went to the bookshelf, I took down the two fat, red volumes, and I plonked them in his lap.

'I'm not sure,' I said. 'I haven't had the courage to count them.'

He glanced down at the two volumes and then looked up at me with real horror on his face.

'Good God!' he said. 'You don't mean to say that *all* these are threatened?'

'Oh, those are only half of them,' I explained. 'Those only deal with the birds and the mammals.'

He was visibly shaken by this, because even today the majority of people do not realize the extent to which we are destroying the world we live in. We are like a set of idiot children, let loose with poison, saw, sickle, shotgun and rifle, in a complex and beautiful garden that we are slowly but surely turning into a barren and infertile desert. It is quite possible that in the last few weeks or so, one mammal, one bird, one reptile, and one plant or tree, have become extinct. I hope not but I know for certain that in the same time one mammal, bird, reptile, and plant or tree, have been driven just that much nearer to oblivion.

The world is as delicate and as complicated as a spider's web, and like a spider's web, if you touch one thread, you send shudders running through all the other threads that make up the web. But we're not just touching the web, we're tearing great holes in it; we're waging a sort of biological war on the world around us. We are felling forests quite unnecessarily and creating dust bowls, and thereby even altering the climate. We are clogging our rivers with industrial filth, and we are now polluting the sea and the air.

When you start talking about conservation, people immediately leap to the conclusion that, as you are an ardent animal lover, what you mean is that you just want to protect the fluffy koala bear or something similar. But conservation doesn't mean this at all. Conservation means preserving the life of the whole world, be it trees or plants, be it even man himself. It is to be remembered that some tribes have been exterminated very successfully in the last few hundred years and that others are being harried to extinction today – the Patagonian Indians, the Eskimoes, and so on. By our thoughtlessness, our greed and our stupidity we will have created, within the next fifty years or perhaps even less, a biological situation whereby we will find it difficult to live in the world at all. We are breeding like rats and this population explosion must be halted in some way. All religious factions, all political factions, the governments of the world, must face facts, for if we persist in ignoring them then, breeding like rats, we will have to die like them also.

Now, though my primary concern is with the conservation of animal life, I am fully aware that you must also conserve the places in which they live, for you can exterminate an animal just as successfully by destroying its environment as with gun or trap or poison. When asked, as I frequently am, why I should concern myself so deeply, I reply that I think the reason is that I have been a very lucky man and throughout my life the world has given me the most enormous pleasure. I feel indebted for it, and I would like to try and do something to repay the debt. People always look at you in a rather embarrassed sort of way when you talk like this, as though you had said something obscene, but I only wish that more people felt that they owed the world a debt and were prepared to do something about it.

Among the numerous letters I get every day there are always those from people who ask me about conservation. They ask whether it is really necessary. Well, as I have just explained, I think it is; I think it is one of the most necessary things in a world full of unnecessary activities, and conservationists are not just making a fuss about nothing. Then I get letters from people who have never, apparently, used their eyes in looking at the world around them. The only thing they understand is figures, because actual figures on paper mean something to them. To this type of person I give figures. And for this purpose the North American continent provides two very good examples of the wastefulness of man.

North America, when it was first discovered by the Europeans, contained two species of creature which were the largest conglomerations of animals that man has known on earth. One of these was the North American buffalo. At first it was killed in order to provide meat. Then it was killed as a deliberate act of policy, in order to try to starve the Indian to death, for it was one of the commodities that he could not do without. The buffalo meant everything to him – even the bones and the hide were of importance to his existence. The much-lauded 'Buffalo Bill' Cody once killed two hundred and fifty buffalo in one day. Passengers travelling in trains through buffalo country had to close the windows for the stench of rotting carcasses because by that time buffaloes were being killed merely for their tongues which were considered a delicacy, and the bodies were left where they fell. Mercifully, the buffalo was saved just in time, but even now we have only a minute remnant of the millions of animals that used to thunder magnificently over the North American prairies.

The second species was the Passenger pigeon, and it was probably the most numerous species of bird that has ever been or ever will be in existence in the world. Flocks of them estimated at two billion used to darken the skies. The weight of their numbers perching in trees could break off quite large branches. It was impossible, everyone thought, that the Passenger pigeon (so delicious to eat and so plentiful) could ever be exterminated. And so they killed and killed; they shot the parent birds, they robbed the nests of the eggs and young. In 1869, seven and a half million birds were captured in one spot. In 1879 a *billion* birds were captured in the state of Michigan. This was because it was

'impossible' to exterminate the Passenger pigeon. It was too numerous. It bred too well.

The last Passenger pigeon in the world died in the Cincinnati zoo in 1914 . . .

Man is clever enough to obliterate a species but he has not, as yet, found a way of re-creating one that he has destroyed. This fact, however, doesn't seem to worry the majority of people. There are even some so-called zoological pundits who say that this is a natural part of evolution and that the animal would have become extinct anyway, with or without our help. I couldn't disagree more violently. To say that it is part of natural evolution is nonsense. It is just begging the question. It is like a man owning a blood bank and saying to somebody who is bleeding to death: 'Oh we've got plenty of blood, old boy, but we can't give you a transfusion because it's in the scheme of things that you should die now.'

'Ah, but,' people say, 'that's what happened in the old days; it doesn't happen now. You've got reserves and so forth where the animals are safe. We don't do that sort of thing nowadays.' To people who believe this I can only quote a few more up-to-date figures to make the picture a little clearer. Every year they 'harvest' – as they call it – between sixty and seventy thousand whales. Although scientists have warned that this exploitation will very shortly make several species of whale extinct and will probably put an end to the whaling industry once and for all, they still continue to do it. It seems that the motto of the whaling industry is: 'Get rich today, and to hell with to-morrow.'

There are many different ways in which an animal can be exterminated and not all of them are simply killing for the sake of clothing or food or because they are considered to be pests. The various species of rhinoceros that were found in the east have been hunted until their numbers are at such a low level that now most of them are only represented by a couple of hundred animals at the most, and the reason for this is the quite stupid belief that the horn, powdered and taken, would act as an aphrodisiac, making the old men virile and attractive to young girls – and this in one of the many parts of the world that is so heavily over-populated that a contraceptive would be more appropriate than an aphrodisiac. Having exterminated practically all the rhinos that were found in India, Sumatra, and Java, they have now turned their attention to the African and, I presume, these will be the next on the list to go down the slippery slopes to extinction.

Let us take the case of the Pacific walrus. When the Eskimoes used them simply as a source of food they utilized the massive tusks to do the most intricate and beautiful carvings. When Eskimo art was 'discovered' by the intelligentsia it became all the rage, and so now the walrus is hunted for its tusks alone and, in fact, is being massacred to such an extent that it will probably shortly be extinct.

It is already on the danger list.

Let us take another example of the clever thinking of sections of mankind, who have no knowledge of nature. In Africa it was decided that the wild-living animals were hosts for the organism that causes Sleeping Sickness. So a brilliant decision was taken: in order to protect man and coddle his scrawny cattle (which were – and are – rapidly eating up all the undergrowth and turning vast areas into dust bowls) it was decided to kill off all the wild animals. Half a million zebras, antelopes, gazelles, and other animals were destroyed before it was discovered that all the smaller animals could also carry the disease. The extermination of this vast quantity of beautiful wild life had therefore been utterly useless.

People get worked up when a couple of thousand human beings per annum are killed on the roads of Great Britain. That is a tragedy of course – but few people know that two million wild birds are killed per annum on the roads, or that in a small area studied by a Danish scientist the number of road deaths were: hares 3,014; hedge-hogs 5,377; rats 11,557; various small mammals 27,834; birds 111,728; amphibians 32,820. These, of course, are only figures for the main roads; if you included the figures for the side roads they would probably be trebled. Now, if human beings were knocked down to that extent in any country in the world there would be such a shriek of protest, such an outcry, such a lamentation, that any government in power would be forced to make us give up the motor car as a means of locomotion and go back to the horse and cart. Not that I'm against the motor car *per se,* but you do see my point?

What is not generally realized is that if you look at a map of the world and see the areas that have been set aside for reserves for wild life, it makes an infinitesimal pinprick on the map; the rest is all a gigantic reserve for mankind. And even if you have reserves, you have to have adequate resources to run them properly. Most governments are reluctant to pay out money for the preservation of habitat or fauna (unless there is some great public outcry and the animal in question happens to be particularly attractive), and many others do not have the necessary resources.

Do not think, for one moment, that I am painting too gloomy a picture. I could go on reeling out these breath-aking statistics for the whole length of this book, and it would only go to prove that, of all the creatures that have ever lived on earth – whether the giant carnivorous reptiles of past ages or the creatures of today – the most rapacious, thoughtless, and blood-thirsty predator is man. And, more-over, he is doing himself irreparable harm by behaving like this. It is suicide; an extraordinary form of Roman death whereby, in bleeding the world white, you kill yourself.

Now, as I said earlier, there are parks and game reserves and so on, but if I may quote from the very excellent book, a quotation from which appears as a heading for this chapter: 'Government protective regulations are meaning-ful only when resources for their effective execution are provided.' We can, perhaps, forgive our ancestors their sins, saying 'They knew not what they did,' but can we – in this technological age that we are so proud of – forgive ourselves for the things we are doing now, and continue to do in the face of opposition from all thinking people whether they be professional zoologists, ecologists, conservationists, or merely thoughtful and perceptive human beings? We have now landed on the moon, and that is a remarkable achievement. But have we gone there just for a few extra minerals, or is the moon to be a great white stepping-stone to other planets, some of which may well harbour their own forms of life? If we are going to go from planet to planet creating the same mess that we have made on our own, then I think it would be a happier thing if the vast sums of money that were spent on space projects were used to try and cure some of the ills that we have inflicted on earth.

The problem of trying to preserve wild life and habitat (both for our own sakes and for the sake of those who will follow us) is a gigantic one, and complicated indeed. There are a great number of countries in the world which, as I have said, give 'paper protection' only to an animal, because the government concerned will pass a law to protect a certain creature but will not allow sufficient funds available so that the reserves – even when they *are* created – are properly controlled and adequately run. In one country I visited I asked what reserves they had, and the man in charge of fauna conservation unrolled an enormous wall map which was covered with green blotches. These, he explained to me proudly, were all reserves. Had they, I inquired in a casual sort of way, been investigated by zoologists or ecologists or biologists, who could tell whether they were, in fact, the most important areas that could be turned into reserves? Oh no, he said, they couldn't afford to do that. Then had investigations been done on these areas, these great green blobs, to find out whether there were, in fact, any animals in them and whether they were suitable as reserves? No, he said, that hadn't been done either, because they lacked the resources to employ the proper people . . . were they, I asked, patrolled in any way? No, he said, they hadn't got the money to have guards or wardens . . . So there was this very fine map, covered in green blotches, which meant nothing at all.

This, as I say, is a common complaint in nearly every country in the world that has any sort of regulation for the preservation of habitat and fauna, and, of course, there are many other countries which have no legislation at all.

This is widely recognized by conservationists and they are doing their best to put the matter right, but it is a slow process. Before we reach the day when the conservation and protection laws are implemented I'm afraid many species will have vanished for ever from the face of the earth.

In most literate countries there are a vast number of clubs, study groups and societies, be they for the ornithologist or for the general naturalist, all trying desperately to do what they can to save their local fauna. On a wider scale you have organizations like the International Union for the Conservation of Nature, The World Wildlife Fund, and so on. In many instances, I'm delighted to say, they have been successful. They have saved, for example, an enormous area of Spain, the Guadalquivir of 625,000 acres. In Australia they rediscovered the Noisy Scrub Bird which had been thought to be extinct. Unfortunately its nesting ground happened to be on a site which had been scheduled for a large new township. Fifteen years ago this would have been considered a most inconsiderate thing for the bird to do and no doubt the township would have been built there, but today the whole thing was replanned in order that the Noisy Scrub Bird should be left in peace and have its own reserve. These are the bright spots; but there are too few bright spots and too many dark ones.

Now, while pressing for conservation of animals in the wild state, there is something else we can do, and that is precisely why I formed my Trust. Many species have been saved from extinction by being taken into zoological gardens or parks and bred under controlled conditions. This, of course, is a last ditch stand, but at least it prevents the species from being completely wiped out and one hopes that, at some future date, the conservation rules and regulations will be enforced in their country of origin so that, having saved a nucleus breeding stock, it will be possible to release them once again to their native area. The list of animals that have been saved in this way is a long and impressive one. There is, for example, the Père David deer which became extinct in China during the Boxer rebellion. Fortunately, the then Duke of Bedford collected together all the Père David deer he could find in the zoological gardens of Europe and released them on his estate at Woburn where they flourished and bred. Now the herd has reached large enough proportions for pairs of this rare deer to be sent to zoos all round the world, and recently they have even been sent back to their place of origin in China. If the Chinese succeed in breeding them – and there is no reason why they shouldn't – they could set aside an area, a reserve, properly patrolled and run, and once more there would be Père David deer in their natural habitat. The Hawaiian goose is another example. This beautiful bird was almost extinct but, due to the sensible attitude of the Hawaiian authorities and the far-sightedness of Peter Scott, it has been saved from certain extinction. There is quite a list of creatures that have been helped in this way, such as the European bison, the North American buffalo, the Saiga antelope, Przewalski's wild horse, and so on, but there are many more that desperately need such help.

The Trust I have created is trying to fulfil exactly this function. I realize that it is merely a cog in the complicated picture of protection today, but we hope that it is an important cog in its own way. It has not been created just to keep the animals in captivity. I look upon it as a reservoir – a kind of stationary ark – in which I hope that we can continue to keep and breed some of the species most urgently in need of protection. Then, at some future date, we can re-introduce them into their original homes. I would gladly see the Trust dissolved tomorrow were there no more need for it. But at present I'm afraid there

is a very great need and I wish I could see similar Trusts springing up all over the world.

As I have explained in this book, I have devoted my life to this work and I have spent a considerable amount of my own money on it, so therefore I do not feel embarrassed at asking you, the reader, if you will help. If you have read this book and enjoyed it; if any of my books have given you pleasure; may I point out that they could never have been written if it had not been for the wild life of the world? Yet all over the world many of these same animals are in a desperate plight and unless they are helped they will vanish. I am trying to do what I can, but I cannot do it without your assistance, so would you please join the Trust, and try and get as many as possible of your friends – or, for that matter, enemies – to join as well? The subscription is low and you can get full information by writing to me at the Jersey Wildlife Preservation Trust, Les Augres Manor, Trinity, Jersey, Channel Islands.

Finally, may I just say that if you don't want to join my Trust, then I beg of you to join some sort of organization that is doing something to try and halt the rape of the world. Do anything you can: worry your local MP – or whatever the equivalent is in your country – into a nervous decline should you think there is going to be some unnecessary, ill-planned encroachment on a valuable piece of habitat, or that some plant or bird or animal is in danger and not receiving sufficient protection. Write indignant letters. It is only by lifting up your voices that the powers that be will be forced to listen. It is worked on the principle that if you shout loud enough and long enough, somebody is bound to hear. Remember that the animals and plants have no MP they can write to; they can't perform sit-down strikes or, indeed, strikes of any sort; they have nobody to speak for them except us, the human beings who share the world with them but do not own it.

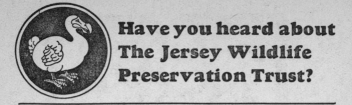

Have you heard about The Jersey Wildlife Preservation Trust?

A special appeal by Gerald Durrell

If you have read my books with pleasure, may I point out that those books would never have been written if it had not been for the wildlife of the world. Now, all over the world, many of these same animals are in a desperate plight and unless they are helped they will vanish for ever. I am trying to do what I can and I want you to help me. If you have enjoyed my writing, if the animals I have described have amused or interested you, then please join my Trust and help in a cause which I believe to be of the utmost importance and urgency.

We need money to create ideal surroundings for the breeding colonies we will establish . . . to provide scientific laboratories so that the animals can be carefully studied . . . to extend and increase the Veterinary Department so that the animals can have the best possible treatment.

You have unfailingly supported me as a writer on wildlife—please support me now in my efforts to save it.

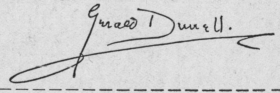

Jersey Wildlife Preservation Trust
Les Augrès Manor, Trinity, Jersey, Channel Islands.
Hon. Director: Gerald Durrell

Please send me details of how I may become a member of the Trust.

NAME (Block letters)

ADDRESS